Which?

25

Consumers' Association 1957-1982

Eirlys Roberts

ISBN 0 85202 241 7
and 0 340 33021 X

Consumers' Association
publishers of *Which?*
14 Buckingham Street
London WC2N 6DS

Photoset by Paston Press, Norwich
Printed in England

Contents

Foreword 5
As it was in the beginning 7
Somewhat later 23
The first quarterly supplement: *Motoring Which?* 41
The *Drug and Therapeutics Bulletin* 45
The second quarterly supplement: *Money Which?* 49
A new director 58
Foreign affairs 60
Hertford: the printers and the subscription department 67
Handyman, holiday and *gardening* 71
The CA laboratory 77
Television and books 83
Research Institute for Consumer Affairs 90
CA's members and non-members 95
Market Intelligence Unit 104
The Survey Unit 107
Towards democracy 110
The five chairmen 117
Campaigning, and the law 122
What's to come 140

Foreword

It can seldom be a good idea to play *Hamlet* without the Prince. But Tom Stoppard, on the fringe of the 1966 Edinburgh Festival, wrote an acclaimed comedy fringing this idea. And now Eirlys Roberts, on the Silver Jubilee of *Which?*, has written about its origins and success this entertaining, highly personal account, whose chief idiosyncrasy is its modest suppression of the pre-eminent role.

Michael Young, our President and initiator, once described Eirlys as "the most considerable figure thrown up by the British consumer movement." *Which?* is her creation. She fitted it out with her own questing mental antennae. For fifteen years and more a toughly intelligent Celtic charm shone from its pages and drew out of those who worked for it more than they thought they had in them.

The legacy endures; for no matter how much Consumers' Association alters, the golden rules of the higher journalism hold good. The information we provide must always be accurate. The way it is communicated must always be accessible. The conclusions we draw from it must always pay regard to the public's interest exclusively.

It is because we stick to these golden rules (give or take a smidgen of human fallibility) that so many rely on us for independent guidance, that the imbalance of power between sellers and buyers has been at least in part redressed, and that after pausing to take stock of twenty-five years' enterprising achievement, we now march on towards a Golden Jubilee even more worth celebrating.

Peter Goldman

As it was in the beginning

We all – well, most of us – believe that Alexander wept because he had no more worlds to conquer, that Edward I held up his infant son to the Welsh, offering them a prince who could speak no word of English, and that Queen Victoria once said dampeningly that 'We are not amused'. In the same way – admittedly, on a more modest level – most of the staff of the Consumers' Association believe that *Which?* was born in a garage in the East End of London, so demonstrating its poor and proletarian origin.

The truth, as so often, is less dramatic. Certainly, Alexander wept, but most likely because the world was so large and he had not yet conquered the half of it. Certainly, Edward made his son Prince of Wales, but not until he was seventeen and – since he was not dumb – could speak English. And Queen Victoria indeed had the character to make that dampening remark, though in fact she did not.

Similarly, *Which?* indeed started life in the East End of London, in a one-room office which had recently been a garage, but which had been lovingly, if inexpertly, decorated and had a typewriter, a table and two chairs.

Which? is now a magazine with a circulation of over 625,000 (and so one of the largest subscription magazines in the country). The organisation which runs it, Consumers' Association, has an income of over £12,000,000 a year, and has many far-reaching changes in the law to its credit. If anyone had prophesied that, twenty-five years ago, the prophesy would have been treated as science fiction. Most of the people who started the organisation half-expected to land up in gaol, or the bankruptcy court, and the future was something they preferred not to think about.

How did we get from there to here?

Over 25 years ago

Remember (or imagine) your fellow-countrymen as they were in the early 1950's: reasonably proud of themselves (they had recently won a war against considerable odds), believing that society could be made much fairer and more equal.

The shops were full of goods, many of them new and exciting, such as washing machines, television sets, dishwashers, ballpoint pens, synthetic textiles, unknown before the war. No-one, however intelligent, was much good at shopping. If they were young housewives, their mothers had probably had jobs during the war and had been too busy to teach their daughters housekeeping. If they were older, they may have remembered shopping before the war when most people could tell the difference between linen and cotton, which is what sheets would be made of, and if you wanted to get something clean, you used soap. Now there were, quite literally, hundreds of different textiles in the shops, labelled, if they were labelled at all, with names no one had ever heard of (what on earth was Trevira?). And there were almost a dozen different brands of things called detergents, all claiming to be the best, and one even going so far as to claim that you didn't need to rinse clothes after using it, for heaven's sake.

Some people, more thoughtful perhaps than the majority, felt puzzled, unconfident and even resentful. They felt that they were entirely at the mercy of manufacturers and advertisers, who clearly knew all about the products they were selling and were

---

From the *London Diary* column in the *Times* 10 April 1980: *Consumers' Association, which can claim to have filled more pages of the statute book than any other pressure group this century, . . .*

---

well able to take the general public – who knew nothing – for whatever ride they chose to.

However thoughtful, most people were not articulate on the subject. Why should they be? They had their lives and their jobs to worry about and it did not occur to them that anything could be changed. Most of the new products were remarkable, and beneficent. Anyone who doubts that should try washing dirty overalls by hand, with yellow soap. If the way washing machines worked, or broke down, was mysterious; if they all looked much the same from the outside but were in the shop at very different prices; if the manufacturers claimed that they performed miracles, and they didn't – then you might complain to your friends, your neighbours or your mother-in-law, but it didn't occur to you that anything could be done about it. It was the way things were, like the weather.

So how did the weather get changed? Not suddenly, but dramatically and astonishingly.

It was changed, obviously, by people who wanted clearer skies and more sun but chose different ways of getting what they wanted – and luck also played a part.

Men in the ministry and women in shops

It goes back to around 1946, when Sir Stafford Cripps as Minister for Economic Affairs set out to tell the general public the facts of the serious economic situation in which the country found itself. There was a campaign of posters (*Export or die, Work or want*) and a unit was set up, first in the Cabinet Office, then in the Treasury, to organise a campaign of publications for industry, trade unions and the general public, and of simple economics lectures to whatever audiences could be induced to listen to them. The head of the unit was Clem Leslie, and Australian who knew how to get a message across to the British public. One of the instruments he chose was Lydia Horton who, at the Ministry of Food during the war had been largely responsible for inducing the English to eat green vegetables. He knew that several million women in this country belong to organisations and he hoped that they would be willing to listen to lectures on the necessity for export, productivity and balancing the national budget.

They were. Lydia Horton collected a committee of the heads of women's organisations to direct the campaign, she and her assistant induced young economists from the Cabinet Office and Treasury (and a few from outside, such as Shirley Williams) to give lectures in basic economics to women's audiences all over England, Scotland and Wales. The audiences took the lectures seriously, drew the logical conclusion that, if Britain was to sell more British goods abroad, foreigners would have to find them worth buying. They realised that foreigners would not necessarily do so, British goods not now being up to the standard of British goods when they were young. This conviction of a rosier past must be at least as old as Cain and Abel and cannot always be justified, but it was deeply felt. The women who held it did not blame other people (the British worker, for instance) but said that they themselves must be largely responsible because, as shoppers, they were ignorant and bewildered and unable to impose on British manufacturers the high standards that their grandmothers had imposed, in a simpler world. The answer to the problem was clearly education and expert guidance of the public.

The young American

Dorothy Goodman was an American postgraduate student in London who had recently married an Englishman. She wanted to install central heating in their new house and asked what was the British equivalent of *Consumer Reports* so that she could find out what was the most reliable, efficient and best value for money in British central heating systems. Her husband's friends gaped. They had never heard of any such thing. It had to be explained to them that, thirty years before, an American engineer from the National Bureau of Standards and an economist had written a book out of which grew, eventually, an organisation called Consumers Union.

These two had pointed out that whenever the U.S. government bought anything, the competing brands were tested first so as to

the very beginning,
in the USA.

THE MACMILLAN COMPANY
NEW YORK · BOSTON · CHICAGO · DALLAS
ATLANTA · SAN FRANCISCO

MACMILLAN & CO., LIMITED
LONDON · BOMBAY · CALCUTTA
MELBOURNE

THE MACMILLAN CO. OF CANADA, LTD.
TORONTO

YOUR MONEY'S WORTH

A STUDY IN THE WASTE OF THE CONSUMER'S DOLLAR

BY
STUART CHASE
AND
F. J. SCHLINK

New York
THE MACMILLAN COMPANY
1927
All rights reserved

be sure that what they were buying was efficient, reliable and the best possible value for the taxpayers' money. So why didn't the government publish the results of what had been found out and let the American public get the best value for their individual money? The U.S. government had not seen it this way (it still doesn't, as far as I know).

Consumers Union was started (at first as Consumers Research; there was a schism and Consumers' Union split off – but that's another story). The subscribers' money was used for testing products so that people who subscribed would know which vacuum cleaner, toaster, radio, perhaps eventually which central heating system to get, thereby saving themselves a great deal of trouble, often a great deal of money. Also, they would have the confident feeling that they had spent their money as well as they could and not been misled by manufacturers, whose interests were different from their own.

Once Dorothy Goodman was convinced that there was no Consumers Union in Britain, she took what – to her – was the obvious step of starting one. Her husband was an economist, director of Political and Economic Planning, an independent research organisation, and his friends tended to be economists, lawyers, civil servants. She enrolled half-a-dozen of them (including Michael Young, sociologist, lawyer and secretary of the research department of the Labour Party), enrolled an engineer (John Thirlwell, from what is now the City University in London)

From *Your Money's Worth* page 252: *If a million citizens could be persuaded to invest one dollar each per year for verified facts about their purchases, wonderful things could be done. In relation to service rendered, scientific work is normally the cheapest thing in the world.*

From *Your Money's Worth* page 3: *We shall plead for an extension of the principle of buying goods according to impartial scientific tests, rather than according to the fanfare and trumpet of the higher salesmanship. This is all. But, as we shall see, it is enough for one book; enough perhaps for a whole shelf of books.*

---

and set them to work producing dummy 'reports' on a few very simple products, such as razor blades.

Unhampered by facts, the reports were fresh and lively, breathing confidence and showing their authors' enjoyment.

The enjoyment soon came to an end. Ray Goodman got a job in the World Bank in Washington, and his wife went with him, leaving Michael Young holding the unborn and unattractive baby, supported only by the small group of the Goodmans' friends, by a certain natural obstinacy, and by a love of new things.

The threat of libel

Against the whole idea was the fact that no one had any spare money, and that they knew that if you wanted to find out what was really in even simple products such as cake-mixes, you would have to put them through a series of expensive tests. There was the fact – everyone believed it was a fact – that although the American public might have the taste and temperament for absorbing a lot of scientific test information and doing their shopping accordingly, the British public certainly would not. Finally – and crucially – everyone knew that English libel laws were different from American libel laws. In America you might be able to say that Tide did *not* wash whiter than any other detergent and get away with it (provided of course that it was true) but if you said the same thing in England you'd find yourself with a whacking libel action, which Procter and Gamble would win.

The first thing that happened was that it occurred to one of the lawyers in the Michael Young group to ask Gerald Gardiner, one of the outstanding lawyers of his time, whether this was true, and he said "No". Under slander of goods, if you can prove that what you say is true, you have nothing to fear. Even if what you say is mistaken but you can show that you said it without malice – and that you have taken every possible precaution to get your facts right, then you have nothing to fear, either.

So what everyone had believed was evidently wrong.

A few dollars more

Then there was money. Michael Young, who came from Australia, had been at school at Dartington Hall, in the community run by the Elmhirsts (Mrs. Elmhirst was an American and they had money) and he had kept close links with them. The Elmgrant Trust gave him £1,000 (later repaid as a loan because *Which?* was not a charity) and Dorothy Goodman, back in the States, extracted about £2,000-worth of dollars from a sympathetic Consumers Union.

So the little group had some money. They advertised for a full-time director at £2,000 a year, which would leave £1,000 for buying and testing an unknown number of products and publishing and printing the results. One has to remember that the group was one of lawyers and economists, not very good at practical finance.

If there is a feeling in the air, not only one person, or one set of people, will breathe it. So, at the same time as Michael Young's group, there were other people – some of them most unexpected – with the same idea.

Shopper's Guide

Elizabeth Gundrey was a journalist on the (now dead, and still mourned) *News Chronicle* who had read *Consumer Reports* and written serious articles about consumer goods. She joined the British Standards Institution's Consumer Advisory Council to edit a magazine called *Shopper's Guide* which would publish tests on the lines of *Consumer Reports*. The British Standards Institution was financed jointly by government and industry, had all the necessary facilities for testing, plenty of money, the authority of an official body and a very good journalist indeed, in Elizabeth Gundrey, to edit the magazine. She (or the BSI for her) had also presumably consulted eminent lawyers who, like Gerald Gardiner, had exploded the myth of the English libel law.

The Observer

In the meantime, Marghanita Laski, the writer (whom no one, I think, except her family, would have thought of as having any domestic interests whatever) had got hold of copies of *Consumer Reports* and had asked her father, Neville Laski Q.C., whether the English libel law would prevent such publications over here. He, too, said "Of course not," and Marghanita Laski wrote two articles for *The Observer* telling people that all aspirin tablets contained exactly the same essential ingredients (so they should buy the cheapest – aspirin BP) and to be aware that bottles of 'orange drink' did not by law need to contain any orange whatsoever.

No one had ever dared to write anything like that before and the articles created a stir. *The Observer* wanted more, but Marghanita Laski's real job was literature, not aspirins, so she suggested that Eirlys Roberts, Lydia Horton's assistant and then successor at the Treasury, should go on with the series in her spare time, if she had any. The Treasury was tolerant (seeing it all as part of the drive for improved British goods) and the articles were written – on products such as detergents, bath salts, cosmetics – in general de-mystifying what was highly advertised and suggesting much cheaper ways of getting the same result. There was, of course, no way of testing the products and the information had to come from interviews with the firms which made them. Their public relations officers were extremely cagey (which Eirlys Roberts, as a Treasury press officer herself, found easy to understand). Their technical departments were almost all extremely frank.

The strands

I have gone into all this detail about what was happening at the time when the British consumers' association started because I believe it is essential to understanding how it happened. The various threads – the British Standards Institution and Elizabeth Gundrey, journalist on a Liberal newspaper; the British Treasury, conscious of the need for having high-quality goods to sell abroad; Marghanita Laski, original and creative; members of women's organisations, conscious of inadequacy in one of their essential roles, as shoppers.

Behind all this – and indeed the material from which the threads were drawn – was the general feeling of ignorance and helplessness on the part of the nation's shoppers and the fact that, after years of austerity during and just after the war, more and more goods were coming into the shops and there was more advertising, including the first television commercials. There was money about and the urge to spend, dammed during the war, burst its banks and flowed over a multitude of objects, some previously rare, some genuinely new. Many people bought with gay abandon. Many others were afraid of being swept away and were prepared to look for any possible raft to which they might cling.

Finally, there was the small group of theoretical people, mainly leftish in sympathy, who seemed to be committed to something which at least the economists among them thought was necessary and which the lawyers thought was not impossible.

Getting organised

This Michael Young group was getting organised. It had a constitution whose Memorandum and Articles of Association declared that its main object was to improve the standard of consumer goods. It had a Council, that is, the members of the group. They all had full-time jobs, so what they needed was a full-time Director, costing not more than £2,000 a year. There were a few replies to their advertisement, and Eirlys Roberts, still at the Treasury and writing the consumer articles for *The Observer* was persuaded to apply. Asked at the interview whether she would like the job, if offered, she said that she could edit their magazine, if they had one, but that they would be out of their minds if they gave her the job of managing anything. Instead of asking, as they well might, why, in that case, she was wasting their time, they said politely that they had to have a director and couldn't afford an editor as well, so perhaps she would like to join the Council, and give her help for free? They employed the same tactics with others, later.

The Council eventually appointed Peta Fordham, journalist, married to a barrister, and allowed her £1,000 to get tests carried out, professionally, on a number of products and the results printed in the form of a magazine.

The first tests

Peta Fordham was precisely what the group needed at that time. She had tremendous energy and a gift for getting people to work for her for nothing, or for very little. She discovered, for instance, that some Public Analysts (local government officials or certain other chemists working on a freelance basis) would report to their authorities on fraudulent or useless or actually harmful branded products in terms that would make your hair curl, but which the press did not pick up. She enrolled one of the most outspoken, the Public Analyst for Birmingham, to analyse various brands of aspirin, very variously priced, to find out what difference in composition, if any, there was between them. She got a private laboratory to test electric kettles; Jack Davey, now a Council member and then, as now, a lecturer at what is now the City University, to organise tests of sunglasses; a group of working wives to bake numerous cakes with various brands of cake mixes; and she induced Council members and their friends to wear brands of non-iron cotton shirts and have them washed under controlled conditions.

The last test was not a success, in spite of the devotion of most of the wearers and their wives. One wearer took his shirts on holiday to Lapland where two of the samples were eaten by reindeer, and one wife insisted on more frequent washing than the test pattern allowed. So the test had to be abandoned.

Early doubts

The other tests went more smoothly but Peta Fordham and the Council had an alarming time. This was the first time that tests like these had been carried out, or even thought of, in this country and who knew what unwitting mistakes you might be making which no one could guess at until they exploded in your face?

If you made no mistakes, one or two eminent lawyers assured you that you would not be sued for libel, but could you really believe them? If you were sued, and lost, would the damages cost every penny the Council members owned? Most of them had a wife and young children. And what was it all for? Everyone knew that the British public would not be interested, and they would never hear about the venture, anyway, because everyone knew that journalists and editors were terrified of their advertising managers and would never report the organisation's uncomfortable findings. Finally, precisely because they believed that their objective was a good one, they feared that, if they tried and failed, no one would take the same risk in this country again – or, at least, not for a very long time.

So why did they persist?

No doubt each would have given a different reason. I believe that all must have shared the feeling of desperation that amateur chess players must sometimes feel when they have sat for half an hour, over the board, so that they make a move though they are sure that it is the wrong one.

The first *Which?*

The magazine was printed at last with mutedly critical reports on brands of electric kettles, sunglasses, scouring powders, cake mixes, aspirins, two cars (reprinted from a Swedish test report), and a think-piece on no-iron cottons (all that remained of the failed shirt test). The Council was happy about the magazine's title *Which?*. It had been suggested by Paul Fletcher, late one night, while everyone got gloomier and gloomier over worthy proposals such as 'Consumer', 'Shopping', 'Value for Money', and it was accepted immediately, with acclaim. But they were happy about nothing else and hired a room at the Waldorf for a press conference, half-hoping that no one would come.

When the day came, the room was packed, with over a hundred journalists, including radio, BBC television, all the national press, including three reporters from *The Times*. The next day, every paper represented carried a report, and by the end of the week the tiny ex-garage in Bethnal Green was awash with envelopes containing 10s note subscriptions to the new magazine. The Council did not know what had hit them.

Take-off

What had hit them was people's need. Here was something which promised to be a guide telling them precisely what to do when faced with the intolerably confusing choice between competing brands, so that they could be certain of making good use of their money, of getting the best value for what they spent. And it was a guide they could rely on because the magazine carried no advertising, on principle, and was to be supported by no money except from its subscribers, certainly not from industry nor even government. The first qualification required of Council members was the negative one that they should have no connection with any trade or business.

This was the obvious practical reason for joining the new organisation. At another level, perhaps mainly unrecognised, was the need to get rid of the feeling of weakness and inferiority to manufacturers and shopkeepers who knew so much more than

---

From *Which?* June 1961 report on drip-dry shirts: *Three and a half years ago, for the first issue of* Which?, *we planned user tests on eight brands of no-iron cotton shirts. Every day for a month, 20 men wore, and their wives washed, one of two shirts, recording their comments daily. At the end of the test period, statisticians went through the records and said, 'These records tell us a great deal about the wearers, but nothing whatever about the shirts.' So we could not use the results. And it is only now that we can fulfil a three-year-old promise and give our members a report based on new tests.*

---

the public about what they were selling. This guide promised to give people the knowledge which would put them on a level with manufacturers, so that they could deal equally with them.

First reactions

Something else that had hit the Council was that they had been entirely wrong about the press, believing them the slaves of their advertising managers. At first – I believe – the journalists and their editors needed courage to support the new magazine as they did. Later on, the relationship between *Which?* and the press became a marriage of great convenience. The press reported *Which?*'s findings but did not mention brand names. This avoided any risk of libel actions or angry advertisers for themselves; and it gave much-needed publicity to *Which?* without giving away the crucial information for which the members paid their subscriptions.

The Council had also been wrong about British manufacturers, who did not, as expected, straightaway attack the infant organisation with libel actions or even letters to the *Financial Times*. Why didn't they? Thinking that *Which?* would fail by itself and that it was better to leave it alone? Unwilling to face the expense and tiresomeness of a court action? Believing that a criticism would soon be forgotten, and if not that a little advertising would soon put it right? Exhilarated by getting noticed, even adversely? Even believing that the venture was a good one, and would benefit industry as well as the public? The Council had no means of knowing since they kept fanatically out of industry's way, refusing the most harmless invitations in case anyone should

---

From the Articles of Association of Consumers' Association: 5. *No person shall be eligible to become or be a member of the Council of the Association if in the opinion of the Council he shall be directly engaged as principal in the manufacture distribution and sale of goods or commodities to or in the rendering of services to the public or shall be directly engaged as a servant or agent in promoting the sales or use of such goods or commodities or services.*

---

suspect that a manufacturer's good dinner would influence his product's rating in *Which?*

In any case, no one had time to ask such questions. They were overwhelmed, first by astonishment, then by the avalanche of envelopes, and for weeks could do nothing except open them, take out the 10s notes and send, in return, the first issue of the magazine with the promise of three more to come. The exercise was organised by Philip Barbour, treasurer of Michael Young's Institute of Community Studies, and carried out by him, his children and any other voluntary help they could enrol. The pillar-boxes for a mile around were stuffed full with *Which?*, until the inhabitants of Bethnal Green complained that they couldn't post their letters, and the Post Office pointed out to the bunch of amateurs that, if they had as many envelopes to send out as this, they could have a special van and why hadn't they just asked?

Philip Barbour was able to hire a few paid staff, none of them ordinary, as clerks or secretaries.

There was Fietje Baukema, for example, who had once ridden for the Dutch team in the Olympics and, in the intervals of checking letters, now rode her bicycle through London traffic to buy electric light bulbs for testing. Edith Rudinger, who took a temporary job in 1957, to help out, and is still with CA now. And Shirley Manning, who had debated, in her bed-sitter, whether to go back home to the Canadian Rockies or apply for this job 'in a grotty office in the East End of London'.

Edith Rudinger, with Michael Young and Philip Barbour and an MP called Wilfred Fienburgh, set up a subscription scheme from the flood of envelopes and had it run professionally by Michael Young's then mother-in-law, who had a secretarial agency. Even so, the ex-garage was now too small and Philip Barbour moved the office (in three trips in his Morris Minor), westwards, to Bloomsbury, not far from Dickens's old house, and near where Dorothy Sayers used to live. The new offices were on the first and second floors. Below them was a society For the Propagation of the Gospel to the Jews which most of the staff noticed, first with surprise that it existed, and then with a fellow-feeling of sympathy for the hardness of their task. But it nearly lost us Lucille Hall, an orthodox Jewish girl, who saw it and walked twice the length of the street before she could bring herself to apply for a job in its proximity. Fortunately for CA, she overcame her scruples. Eventually she became CA's press officer, propagating the consumer gospel.

In the meantime, Peta Fordham had resigned, disagreeing with the Council, not on principles but on emphases. They thought her too much of a journalist, too little a scientist, while she (no doubt) found them unworldly and pernickety.

Somewhat later

So Michael Young took over as Director until one could be appointed, with Eirlys Roberts as Editor. The organisation, which before the first issue of *Which?* came out had had debts of £187, had 10,000 members paying 10s each the week after, so it could now afford both a Director and an Editor. Some of the Council members must have felt relief, and even pleasure. The editor was only conscious that the first issue had taken a year to produce and the second must be out in six weeks, and be even better.

The Times have said that the readers' letters are the best-written and most interesting part of the paper. This may be so, but *The Times*'s debt to its readers cannot compare with *Which?*'s debt.

The members

I cannot think of any paper or magazine which owed (and owes), so much to its member-readers as *Which?* It was not that they wrote it, and *Which?* rarely published their letters. But they offered, free, the benefit of their experience and expertise, and it is hard to see how *Which?* could have managed at all without them.

The second issue of *Which?* published a breakdown of the first 10,000 members, by sex, concluding cautiously (and unwillingly because most people assumed that they would be women) that the majority were men; and by occupation. Most professional people (not others) named their occupation and included at the – numerically – bottom end 1 bishop, 1 High Commissioner, 1 ex-Cabinet Minister, 1 judge and 1 sculptor and, at the top, 203 doctors. In the middle were 65 Army, 31 Navy and 29 RAF officers, 32 clergymen, and a sprinkling of chemists, engineers, teachers and dentists. Many of them offered their help and many of the offers were accepted.

Members who were professional chemists analysed drugs, proving, for example, that the different brands of stomach powder that were tested, whose prices varied from 6d to 2s 8d an oz, contained the same ingredients, and doctors were willing to state, for publication, that anyone who bought any except the cheapest was a fool. A professor of dentistry organised tests on toothpastes, stripping away the claims of advertising. A physicist from Harwell rigged up a machine to make 21 ballpoint pens do 130 miles of writing. Naval officers, later, and coastguards helped to test sailing dinghies and life-jackets. Home economists from London University made sponge-cakes to test gas ovens. All these were specialists who had known or suspected for years what the tests were proving, and felt strongly about the misled public. *Which?* was the way in which they could relieve their feelings.

The doctors in particular relieved their feelings with a forthrightness that made the Editor pale. "We can't possibly put it like that. Michael Rubinstein would have a fit."

No libel if you are right

Michael Rubinstein was and is CA's libel lawyer and a draft of every report was and is sent to him before publication.

He was not, in fact, given to having fits. His comments came back with a certain sameness: "If you are absolutely sure that you are accurate in saying that that electric kettle is unsafe (or that the paint on a child's toy is full of lead or Queen Bee jelly won't make you live longer), then there is no risk of libel. If not, God help you. And, by the way, the syntax of the last paragraph on page 2 . . .".

"Fat lot of help that is," the Editor would mutter, "and I wish he would stick to his law and leave our syntax alone."

Of course, he was right. What *Which?* had to do was to be sure beyond doubt that its every sentence was accurate, that every possible step had been taken to see that it was so, and that no bias for or against any product or manufacturer, or for or against manufacturers in general, had affected any statement or the way in which it was written.

Which? would not claim that this was virtuous behaviour. If we made a criticism that turned out to be wrong, we ran the risk – as Michael Rubinstein said – of a libel action, and a libel action at that stage would have destroyed the organisation. More important, if we had been inaccurate, there would soon have been no organisation to destroy. All that *Which?* was offering its members in return for their subscriptions was information which, if accurate, would be useful to them. If it had not been accurate it would not have been useful, and the organisation would have ceased to exist.

To some extent, this need for accuracy conditioned the language used in *Which?*. If you know for certain that no detergent washes whiter than any other or that doctors do not all recommend Wright's Coal Tar soap, then you can say so, without qualification or hesitation and with complete clarity. In fact, you had better. What is important, for the law and for your members, is not what you meant to write, but what they understand by what you write. So you make sure that there is no doubt about what you mean.

Another reason for clarity was the ignorance of most technical and scientific matters shared by the *Which?* editorial staff and CA's members. Some might be specialists in photography or electronics or chemistry or electrical engineering, but very few could be specialists in more than one subject. Consumer goods cover all subjects, so the *Which?* project officers had to find out about the subjects of which they were ignorant – say, photography when they were describing tests on cameras or chemistry when on bath salts – and to convey the results of the tests, and as much of the theory of the subject as they thought necessary, to their equally ignorant members. The exercise made for clarity.

Eirlys Roberts, 1957, before she was Editor of *Which?*

Simple words

There was another, accidental, reason for the simple language of *Which?*. The Editor, and later on the deputy editor, Maurice Healy, and a deputy research director had all happened to read classics at their school and university. A good teacher will require that a Latin or Greek text shall be translated into Anglo-Saxon words – how else will they know that a pupil who translates *mare caeruleum* as cerulean sea knows what colour that is?

So the *Which?* project officers were required to use concrete nouns, not abstract ones, the active not the passive voice, short sentences, short paragraphs and short, Anglo-Saxon words. They did so, and as far as I can remember there was only one successful rebellion when the project officers said that the Editor might carry out the unscientific process of *choosing* a sample but that what they did was scientifically to *select* it.

Which?'s style was also familiar, addressing the readers as 'you'. This arose naturally from a feeling of mutual involvement. In return, the readers, who often helped with user tests and wrote letters with comments and criticism by the thousand, often used 'we' when addressing the magazine – "We really ought to have reported on more brands of electric heaters in the last issue", "We pulled our punches on that one, didn't we?"

Some early *Which?* people

When CA could afford a director, they appointed Caspar Brook who came from the Economist Intelligence Unit, and had business experience which the Council lacked. He was dynamic, brave and a good administrator.

Caspar laid it down that everyone, from himself to the caretaker, should be known by his or her Christian name, which was unusual at the time and caused confusion when someone rang up for, say, Mr. Brook and was asked "Mr. *Who*?"

I suppose that the history of most organisations is the history of the people who worked for them. It was particularly true of

Which?, since so many of them were personalities, in very different ways.

Eric Tolton came to CA from being a Labour Party agent in Lowestoft, years ago, a career which teaches you how to deal with problems. Eric has been dealing with CA's practical problems ever since, organising office moves, shifting people around inside offices, transporting goods to and from Europe for the European Testing Group, quick on his feet. He's the sort of person who not only knows how your immediate difficulty can be overcome but overcomes it for you. This is not recommended as the route to high office, but it earns the respect – even love – of one's fellow workers.

Another one of the early arrivals was Jeremy Mitchell, young, tall, blond, who looked like an athlete, was an economist with the mind of a scientist, and a calm, measured way of speaking. In any discussion he tended to say nothing until the end when he would come out with his opinion, which won. He was made deputy research director, was responsible for administering the tests and the project officers and – looking back – it is difficult to see how the early *Which?* could have survived without him.

Two of the earliest project officers to arrive were Gerald Bailey and Michael Dunne. Project officers were usually young (*Which?* could not afford high salaries), usually required to have a university degree and some experience of the working world, but the only essential requirement was that they should be able to distinguish between what was evidence and what was not. *Which?* prized these two particularly because, in addition, they had worked in plastics and aircraft engineering respectively and so had the technical expertise which the rest of the staff conspicuously lacked.

Maurice Healy, Irish, classics at Cambridge, just started on a promising career in the Minister's Private Office in the Board of

---

From CA's Annual Report for year ended 31 March 1960: *The move to 333 High Holborn made possible the establishment of a general office. The office manager, Mr. Eric Tolton, and his staff have greatly helped other departments to function efficiently, often under pressure of printers' and other deadlines.*

left: in the 1960's, Caspar Brook.

below left: Jeremy Mitchell, then deputy research director, *Which?*, now the director of the National Consumer Council.

below right: Maurice Healy.

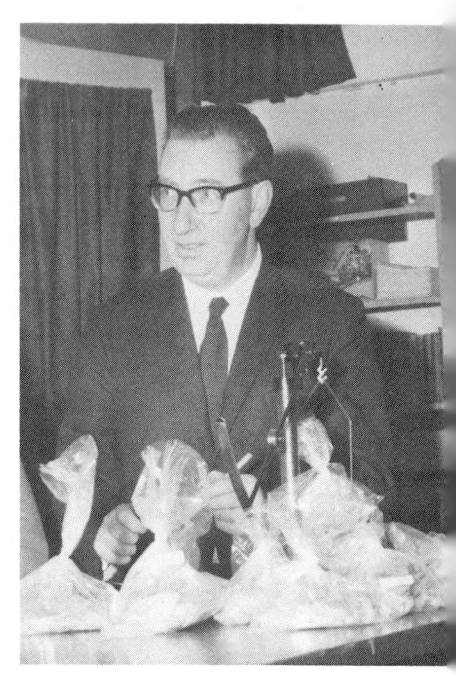

above left: Eric Tolton.

above right: Gerald Bailey in 1966, taking part in a 'how many chips for sixpence?' project for his local consumer group.

right: Daphne Grose, then as now gathering and giving information.

Trade, applied for a job as a project officer. He was told most earnestly that he must be mad. The Civil Service offered certain security, *Which?* almost certain disaster and that, before disaster fell, he would find himself doing things which the Civil Service would not consider dignified. The first of these, when he turned down the good advice, was a test of picnic stoves, part of which he had to re-do on the floor of his office when the lab test went wrong. His report ended with the gratuitous finding that, to light a fire under a picnic kettle, the *Daily Worker* and the *Daily Telegraph* were two of the Best Buys and *Which?* itself NOT RECOMMENDED. His career in CA thereafter was steadily upward, ending as editor in chief.

Most of the project officers' work consisted of asking the questions members wanted answering, and finding the answer. The staff was spoilt from the beginning because they had another young civil servant – from the Monopolies and Mergers Commission – as librarian. Daphne Grose was the kind of librarian who had little need of books. She had most of the facts in her head. And when she had not, although apparently shy, seemed not to mind ringing people up and asking for what might seem outlandish information. There were surprises in both directions. When she rang a university department specialising in transport to ask for the comparative costs of running one kilometre of railway line in six different countries, there was a shout of laughter at the other end of the phone and she was told that if she liked to come along and spend four years with them, she might find the answer and, if she did, they'd give her a Ph.D. On the other hand, when, for a report on women's shoes, she was asked to find out what was the pressure in pounds per square inch of an elephant standing on one foot, and she rang the zoo with a slightly sick feeling in her stomach, "African or Asian?" asked the voice at the other end.

Checking and verifying

Caspar Brook invented a system of checkers, verifiers and data checking sheets for the *Which?* reports.

Checkers were people not on the staff, experts in special

Portable typewriters being tested for the August 1973 issue of *Which?*

Testing toothbrushes for Autumn 1958 *Which?* on a machine in which twelve hours gave the brushes the kind of wear that a year's twice-daily use would give them.

Egg beaters on a wear-test machine, for Winter 1959 *Which?*

The earliest ballpoint pens wear-test machine in 1958 was built of Meccano. This rig was constructed for the report on fibre tip pens in *Which?* May 1971.

subjects, interested *Which?* members, housewives, and also Council members, who were sent the first draft of reports. Their comments and criticism saved us from much foolishness and their help was beyond price (literally also, because it was years before *Which?* could afford to pay them more than a nominal fee). On the whole, the comments, if astringent, were polite, though one project officer was known to have gone home for the day, wounded by the comments on one of his reports.

Jokes did not survive. When half a dozen people have said that a joke is not funny, you take it out.

Verifiers on the staff had the job of taking a project officer's report and checking every fact in it. I often wondered how the girls amongst them managed it – spending the working day questioning the accuracy of facts painfully garnered by often arrogant young men and dealing with often irate manufacturers. Anyway, they did manage it and they knew that they were doing one of the most important jobs in *Which?*, however little credit they might get from the smarting project officers. Alisdair Aird and Joan Meier were two of the toughest verifiers before being promoted motoring editor and car project officer respectively.

I should mention Shirley Manning particularly. She was the first of the verifiers and for a long time the only one, and set the standard for those who followed. She insisted on questioning the smallest facts ("does Woolworth's spell itself apostrophe s or is it Woolworths' or Woolworth?") but was more interested in the concepts governing the research. At 1 a.m. on OK-press day, with the printers hovering, she would question whether the

---

From *Which?* April 1959, page 3: *This is the first monthly issue of* Which?. *We have decided to bring* Which? *out every month, instead of every quarter, mainly because many of our members have asked for it. And we are glad to do so, chiefly because it means that we can be more topical. If we had planned a report on, say, sun-tan lotions for June and something held it up (tests having to be re-done, for instance) the report wouldn't be much use in September. But in July, it still would be.*

At the same time, as we tell you in our letter, the subscription has been raised from 10s to £1.

---

decibel rating of the noise made by a vacuum cleaner was any real measurement of the irritation caused to the woman who was using it. The editor and project officer, worn out, would say that it was certainly no measurement of the irritation she was causing them, but more often than not she was right and they had to give way. The following month she would be at it again, querying the size of a sample in a survey, the inherent likelihood of a lab result, the necessity for giving so much detail about a record-player – surely, all that our members wanted to know was what it sounded like and how likely it was to go wrong.

Such persistence needed courage as well as conviction, and project officer and editor knew its value, however fractious they might get.

Data checking sheets are sent to the manufacturers of the products reported on. They contain no test results of other manufacturers' products and no judgments, but any serious failure (eg of a British Standard) is mentioned so that the manufacturer has a chance to explain the failure, if he can, and so that there could re a re-test if necessary.

All this was in the interests of accuracy. When the accuracy broke down – or when a manufacturer thought it had – he wrote, telephoned or called immediately, usually threatening to sue the editor, the publisher and the printers. If these letters had all been given to the project officers or editor to answer, I do not think they could have survived. Knowing this, Caspar appointed a Scotsman called Alastair Macgeorge to do the answering. I doubt whether Alastair ever got the gratitude he deserved from the editorial staff but the director has no doubt of his value. He has shifted him around ever since to go where trouble is, and put it right.

Not only triumphs

There is a natural tendency, I suppose, to remember success rather than disasters. So, looking back, one sees a smooth progression of reports compiled with great care, meticulously verified (and I mean 'meticulous' literally, careful with the fear of being wrong) and passing free of trouble into print.

CONSUMERS' ASSOCIATION LTD publishers of **Which?**

7 Great James Street · London WC1 · CHAncery 3593

190/Pr.6

P R E S S   R E L E A S E

Thursday 30th October 1958

"W H I C H ?" No. 5

is published from

7 Great James Street London W C 1.

For some time, there has been a certain amount of confusion between two names - our own, Association for Consumer Research Limited, and that of a Company carrying out market research for business firms - Consumer Research Limited. Consumer Research Limited recently announced a scheme for carrying out tests on clients' products and awarding a seal ("APPROVED BY CR") if the tests were passed. Since manufacturers sometimes ask us to carry out such tests for them and are always refused, it was clear that the risk of confusion was increased. We therefore met Consumer Research Limited to discuss what could be done to remove this risk. We proposed (amongst other things) that they should abandon their approval scheme, and that we should change our name from Association for Consumer Research Limited to Consumers' Association Limited.

The aims and purpose of the Association, whose revenue continues to derive from members' subscriptions, remains unchanged - to undertake stringent tests of goods and services available to the ordinary consumer, and to report the results in "W H I C H?".

CONSUMERS' ASSOCIATION LTD publishers of Which?

7 Great James Street · London WC1 · CHAncery 3593

PRESS RELEASE

"W H I C H?" No 6, the winter 1959 issue of the quarterly published from 7 Great James Street London W.C.1. is being mailed to the 110,000 members of the Consumers' Association Limited on Monday January 19th 1959

Since "W H I C H?" No 5 was published on 31st October 1958, the Association's membership has grown by over 25,000. Of these, 7,000 received their associate membership as a Christmas gift from enthusiastic existing members.

A milestone in the short life of the Consumers' Association was reached at the beginning of December when the 100,000th member, Mrs Harrison of Oxford, joined CA.

The print order for "WHICH?" No 6 is 150,000.

All enquiries to Miss Rudinger - CHAncery 3593.

14/PR/1

This is not always so. Very early on, we published a report on soot-destroyers – things which were put on the fire to get rid of the soot in your chimney so that you did not need to have it cleaned by a sweep. The report was quite a simple one (after analysing them, *Which?* was sceptical about their effectiveness). Unfortunately, after the report had been written and edited, the suggestion that you would get the same result if you put an old dry battery on the fire instead was added in the printed report. It was then discovered that if you did any such thing, the battery might explode. So over 100,000 *Which?* members were sent a postcard entreating them to pay no attention to that bit of the report and keep batteries well away from the fire.

Then there was the lead content of frying pans. *Which?* tested a number of them, adding some baking tins; lead in the lining of a pan could get into any food cooked in it, and, if there were too much, would be unsafe. The laboratory reported that one of the baking tins had a lead content slightly over the British Standard limit. The verifier accepted the laboratory report and the figure was included in *Which?*. The laboratory report was wrong and *Which?* settled with the manufacturer in open court and printed an apology.

The most troublesome – and in a way, frightening – of these cases was that involving a brand of car seat belts. There was at the time (and still is) a British Standard test for car safety belts which includes various tests for the strength and performance of the seat and buckle, carried out on a rig with a dummy that simulated actual crashes. The Dutch State Laboratory carried out similar tests. For a number of technical and practical reasons, *Which?* decided to have the seat belts tested on the Dutch rig and sent batches of the belts to be tested in the Netherlands. Buckles on four out of fifteen samples of one of the most-sold British seat belts failed the crash tests at a level which was equivalent to the BS requirements. Since the belts had been approved by the BSI, an argument with the manufacturer about the relative validity of the *Which?* tests and those done by BSI continued for over two years. One important factor which affected the performance of the buckles was the amount of slack in the belt when it was tested. *Which?* remained convinced that its tests were fair, the

CONSUMERS' ASSOCIATION LTD publishers of Which?

7 Great James Street · London WC1 · CHAncery 3593

29/eer/8

PRESS RELEASE

for 4th February 1959

BREAKING UP DRY BATTERIES

The report on soot destroyers in "W H I C H?" No 6 (published by the Consumers' Association) describes how they work and what they are made of - mixtures of common salt and metallic salts such as copper sulphate, zinc sulphate, ammonium chloride. Their effectiveness in cleaning flues and chimneys is compared with that of throwing common salt on the fire.

As dry batteries contain zinc and ammonium chloride, "WHICH?" suggested that an old dry battery might be broken up and put on a hot fire to reduce soot in the chimney.

The source of CA's statement was a U.S. Bureau of Mines Report, which stated that the practice was prevalent in the U.S.A. and that their tests showed that it might be effective. Neither the U.S. Bureau of Mines Report, nor the fuel technologists of unquestionable authority whom the Consumers' Association had also consulted before publishing the report in "WHICH?", indicated that from the safety point of view it is essential that the battery be broken up.

Since publication, it has been drawn to CA's attention that if dry batteries are not broken up before being put on the fire, there is a danger that they might explode. Although the extent of the risk is not known, in the interests of its members and other readers of "WHICH?", the Consumers' Association thought it right to send out a postcard emphasising that the dry battery must be broken up.

Enquiries to Miss Rudinger - CHAncery 3593.

manufacturer remained convinced that they were not. In the end, a statement in open court made it clear that *Which?* did not suggest that the safety belts did not conform to the British Standard, the manufacturer did not suggest that *Which?*, in deciding to have the tests carried out in the Netherlands, had any motive except concern for public safety, and both sides paid their own costs.

The first quarterly supplement: *Motoring Which?*

The director, unlike the editor, loved cars and realised that many of *Which?*'s mostly male members would probably be interested enough in tests on cars to subscribe to extended reports in a separate magazine. So *Which?* advertised for a car tester, and the director and editor were faced with two final candidates. One was Dick Nutt, a studious engineer, who loved engineering, and Ray Nunwick, ex-vehicle accident inspector in the police, who loved cars, climbing, potholing, foreign food and stiff discipline. Faced with an impossible choice, they decided to hire both, Dick Nutt as chief car tester, Ray Nunwick as his deputy. No doubt this broke rules of good management. There is no doubt whatever that the partnership was one of *Which?*'s greatest successes.

CA rented an ex-airfield in Essex and re-asphalted the runway to use as a test-track. Dick and Ray set up an office and workshop

---

From *CA News* in *Which?* January 1962: *In this issue,* Which? *produces, for car subscribers, its first report on cars. In a way, we are sad not to be able to include reports on cars in the ordinary* Which?, *but the 15% of members who asked us to test cars gave us clear directions not to do so at the expense of the rest of our testing programme. Since buying and testing cars is enormously expensive, as you can imagine, the only solution was to have separate subscriptions. And we are encouraged that nearly 70,000 of our members have already decided to take out car subscriptions.*

---

in the ex-control tower, hired driver-mechanics, and started testing cars and fighting the car project officer and editor back in London. Every quarter the Car Test Unit collected thousands of facts – all verified – about a group of cars. They had sweated for months to collect them and written every one down for the benefit of the subscribers. Every quarter Ray failed to understand why the car project officer should have to cut so many of them out. "We can only get so many words on a page", he or she would say despairingly, "And even if we had more pages the readers don't need all those facts to choose one car."

The reports in *Motoring Which?* were different from anything that had been written about cars before in this country. They were comparative, reporting not on one car but on the choice that faced the car buyer – half a dozen or more cars of the same size and type. They were objective – based on workshop and laboratory tests, not the subjective opinion of one driver. The cars were driven a long way – 10,000 miles, in varying conditions. And *Motoring Which?* had no hesitation in pointing out serious faults, unlike other motoring journals which tended to praise everything except the ashtrays. The readers liked this.

British car manufacturers, on the other hand, did not like *Motoring Which?*. The first issue found that the German Volkswagen was the best car in its group and later issues often found that foreign cars were more reliable, or better value in some other way, than British ones, and said so. There were complaints – not only from car manufacturers – that these reports were unpatriotic because they stopped people buying British cars. *Which?* was unmoved. We knew that we were helping the members by giving them the facts for which they paid. And CA had been established to raise the standard of British goods by telling the truth about them. This was the aim, with cars too.

It is difficult – maybe impossible – to convey the spirit of that early Car Test Unit. They were half a dozen young technicians, led by one introvert engineer and one extravert disciplinarian, working under the open Essex skies, beautiful to those who like that kind of scenery, cut off from the office in London, keeping puritanical standards in the way they did their job, and believing themselves the most important part of the organisation. In this,

At CA's car test unit, in 1962. Frank Jones and the editor. He is now senior tests engineer at Gosfield.

for *Motoring Which?*, July 1965, 'poorly supported front luggage compartment lid . . .'

they were no different from anyone else (it was one of *Which?*'s strengths that *everyone* believed him or herself to be the most important person in the organisation). But they differed from the Londoners in being uninterested in consumer philosophy, and in a maleness so exclusive that for some time even their secretary was a man. But two women-drivers were hired on a freelance basis.

Part of the cars' testing programme was a 'rough ride' of some 1,000 miles over the Pennines, into Scotland and back again to Essex. The editor joined them once on Loch Lomond (a female boss was accepted if a secretary was not) and will never forget the November ride over the hills of Galloway dusted with snow, the mutterings of the drivers, obliged by Ray to stop every so many miles to fill in their fact sheets.

The 'new and improved' Motoring Which? *superseded car supplements in July 1965. From CA Annual Report for the year ended 31 March 1966:* Motoring Which? *got off to a good start in July by publishing, in addition to car reports, articles on car defects (based on a survey by the Research Institute for Consumer Affairs) and tyre pressure gauges. Subsequent issues have had articles on car prices, new and secondhand, and a major contribution to the debate on car safety.*

The *Drug and Therapeutics Bulletin*

The first director of Consumers Union in the United States was Arthur Kallett who later, after he had left CU, started the *Medical Letter*, a publication for doctors, to give them the same detached and unbiased (though untested) information about drugs that *Consumer Reports* gave CU's members about products in general. The *Medical Letter* was highly thought of in the States; drugs (because of their cost and the harm they could do) had always been a subject of concern to CA. In 1962, CA decided to publish a British version and appointed, as editor, Dr. Andrew Herxheimer, then of the London Hospital, whose speciality was pharmacology. A four page British edition has come out fortnightly ever since. At first all the material was of American origin, edited for British readers; gradually more original material was introduced and since 1963 the *Drug and Therapeutics Bulletin* has been entirely British. An advisory council gives its advice, some 30 specialists comment on the draft articles, and the manufacturers of any drug named is also asked for comment on what is said about it.

I do not think that people in general realise the extent to which doctors – and dentists and pharmacists – are inundated with advertising material about drugs, particularly new ones. They could not possibly get the time to assess it all and, if they had the time, could not possibly have the necessary scope of specialist knowledge. So the *Drug and Therapeutics Bulletin* does the assessment for them, appraises manufacturers' claims, summarizes the research into new drugs, compares them with existing ones, and gives the clear and unequivocal conclusions which are possible only when everything has been looked at and all the work done.

It now has a circulation of 73,000.

THE MEDICAL LETTER

a non-profit-making publication on Drugs and Therapeutics

Published by Consumers' Association Ltd. and based on material supplied by Drug and Therapeutic Information, Inc., New York

Vol. 1, No. 1 British Edition April 20, 1962

MORPHINE AND PETHIDINE

Except for codeine, pethidine is the most widely used of all narcotics. It was synthesized in 1939 in a search for new spasmolytic drugs of the atropine type. Its analgesic properties then came to light; but the notion that the drug is spasmolytic, anti-colic, or relaxant to smooth muscle, has been persistent. It was also believed at first to be more analgesic, less addicting, and less prone to cause nausea, vomiting and respiratory depression than morphine. All of these impressions were formed at a time when it was often assumed that pharmacological effects in animals would necessarily occur in man; and when the principles of the controlled clinical trial were not widely understood.

PROBLEM OF DOSAGE - Considerable confusion in judging the relative analgesic, sedative and side effects of morphine and pethidine arises out of the failure to compare the drugs in equi-analgesic doses and by the same route of administration, whether parenteral or oral. Examination of the few substantial studies of the drug which are available does not bear out the superiority of pethidine over morphine in any important respect, and there have been no more recent studies that would change the picture.

Pethidine in doses of about 75 mg. parenterally provides effective analgesia of the same duration as about 10 mg. of morphine. Although "morphine gr. 1/4" is frequently prescribed, 16 mg. is generally an excessive dose, with consequent increase in side effects; the optimal dose in most cases is 10 mg. (L. C. Lasagna and H. K. Beecher, J. Amer. med. Ass., 1954, 156, 230).

RESPIRATORY DEPRESSION - It is often said of pethidine that unlike morphine it does not much depress respiration; but this difference is not borne out by studies with equivalent doses. Well-controlled studies have shown that they do so equally when equivalent therapeutic doses are used. In obstetrical analgesia the respiratory depression caused by both drugs is a definite hazard to the newborn. Respiratory depression also continues to be an important problem in the care of seriously ill postoperative patients. A relaxing effect of pethidine on bronchial smooth muscle has not been demonstrated in vivo, and clinicians still differ as to whether either morphine or pethidine has merits sufficient to offset the hazard of respiratory depression in relieving acute asthmatic attacks not responsive to usual measures. For the relief of acute left ventricular failure and pulmonary oedema, pethidine has not been shown to have any

Fortnightly for doctors
from the publishers of **Which?**

ISSN 0012-6543

Volume 20 No.16
August 6 1982

drug and therapeutics bulletin

NETILMICIN: A NEW AMINOGLYCOSIDE ANTIBIOTIC

Netilmicin (Netillin - Kirby Warrick) is a semi-synthetic aminoglycoside which is structurally related to gentamicin. The manufacturer claims that it is less toxic and has a wider spectrum of activity than gentamicin.

Spectrum - Netilmicin, like gentamicin, tobramycin and amikacin, is active against most strains of E.coli, Klebsiella, Enterobacter, Proteus, Serratia and Staph.aureus, but not against streptococci and anaerobes.[1] It is less active against Pseudomonas than the other aminoglycosides. Like amikacin, netilmicin is stable to bacterial adenylases and phosphorylases mediating resistance to gentamicin and tobramycin, but, unlike amikacin, is inactivated by most of the bacterial acetylases which destroy gentamicin and tobramycin.[2,3] The proportion of gentamicin-resistant strains which are susceptible to netilmicin will vary with the local prevalence of bacteria with the different drug-destroying enzymes. Netilmicin was active against about 60% of over 1,400 gentamicin-resistant strains collected mainly from North and South America.[1] Activity against gentamicin-resistant organisms is unlikely to be generally useful in this country at present as gentamicin resistance is uncommon. However, in units where it is a problem the prevalent strains should be tested for susceptibility to netilmicin.

Pharmacokinetics - Netilmicin, like all aminoglycosides, is not absorbed when given by mouth and must be given by injection. The drug is excreted by glomerular filtration and in adults with normal renal function its elimination half-life in serum is about 2½ hours. Netilmicin can be detected in tissues, sputum, and peritoneal, pleural and joint fluids in concentrations 25-50% of those in serum. Like all aminoglycosides, netilmicin enters the cerebrospinal fluid poorly even when the meninges are inflamed.[4] In patients with renal failure or in premature babies,[5] the half-life of netilmicin is prolonged.

Dosage - In adults and children the manufacturer recommends 2 to 2.5 mg/kg 8-hourly or in adults up to 3 mg/kg 12-hourly i.m. or i.v. Experience with the 12-hourly dosage is still too limited to recommend this schedule for severe infections. Twice daily dosage is used for amikacin and kanamycin and in theory could also be used for gentamicin and tobramycin.

Toxicity - In animals netilmicin is substantially less nephrotoxic than gentamicin, tobramycin and amikacin,[6] and less ototoxic than gentamicin and amikacin.[7-9] In man netilmicin trough levels of 3 mg/l and peak levels of 15 mg/l caused no toxicity,[10] with trough levels greater than 3 mg/l renal function was transiently worsened.[11] In a review of published

Eirlys Roberts at Smithfield Market. There were reports on meat labelling in *Which?* April 1971 and 1972.

Tim Crawley-Boevey, when editor of *Money Which?*

The second quarterly supplement: *Money Which?*

Money Which? was the next enterprise and the editor was there, ready-made. Tim Crawley-Boevey, Cambridge (English), Durham Light Infantry (national service), and work with a shipping agent, had started off as a project officer on television sets and stereo equipment, and then moved on to a supplement on Contraceptives.

The contraceptives supplement

Perhaps we should go back first to *Contraceptives*. It is difficult, in 1982, to remember why we should have felt so apprehensive, in 1963, about reporting on this subject. It was suggested by Mary Adams, a Council member, who had been head of BBC Television Talks, and the editorial department was not enthusiastic. This time it was not the thought of libel that worried them, nor even the susceptibilities of the shoppers who would have to go round buying the things in hundreds. But what would be the feelings of our members? Even more immediately, what would be the feelings of Jeremy Mitchell, by this time deputy research director, and James Douglas, a valued Council member, both Roman Catholics? We were wrong to worry about them, as Protestants often are about Roman Catholics. Our members bought thousands of copies of the Supplement, written in Tim's cool prose, and only a handful complained.

We had a slight contretemps with one of the newspapers. Before the Supplement was published we sent them an advertisement for it, accepted by all except the *Daily Mirror*, who refused on the grounds that they could not accept such an advertisement as they were a family newspaper. After publication, the *Daily Mirror* gave the Supplement a double page centre spread, possibly the most full and accurate of all the press reports. So CA wrote to the *Mirror* suggesting that perhaps now they might be willing to take the advertisement. "Certainly not'" said the *Mirror*. "Don't you realise that we are a family newspaper?"

Money Which?

Anyway, Tim followed up the success of the Contraceptives Supplement with another on life insurance and then became editor of the new quarterly *Money Which?*

It took *Which?* and its members quite a while to realise that people need help if they are to get value for money when they buy services as well as when they buy goods. That you can make a big enough mistake when you buy the wrong washing machine (paying an unnecessary £30, say) but a much larger one when you buy the wrong life insurance policy (£2,000 *Money Which?* found, in one report). Even more important, money

---

From CA's Annual Report for year ended 31 March 1961: *In January 1961 we moved into more spacious premises – our fourth address in less than four years. Overcrowding at High Holborn had reached a stage at which efficiency was being affected adversely and development impeded.*

From *A brief history of number fourteen Buckingham Street* by Jonathan Miller, p. 29: *By some mysterious urbane alchemy, Number 14 has always attracted tenants that typify their era: bishops, courtiers, politicians, bureaucrats, artists, scientists, writers, and business men. Their story casts an oblique light on English history, highlighting unfamilar features and also foreshadowing the future. In the same tradition Consumers' Association, with its useful service and popular and informal organisation, may also be a significant omen for our property owning democracy.*

PRESS RELEASE

Which?

Consumers' Association
14 Buckingham Street
London WC2
01-839 1222

For publication on or after:	Sunday, January 11, 1970	Inquiries to:	LUCILLE HALL 01.839.1222

The Which? Contraceptives Supplement, published on Monday, January 12, 1970, costs 15s through booksellers or from Consumers' Association, 14 Buckingham Street, London, WC 2

==

Because of the general need for independent information on this subject, Consumers' Association is making this Which? Supplement available to anyone; it is not necessary to be a subscriber to Which?

==

Consumers' Association has sold over 180,000 copies of its report on contraceptives since the first one appeared in 1963. New tests were carried out for this edition, which is completely revised and brought up-to-date in the light of current knowledge.

For the Contraceptives Supplement the Which? shoppers bought, anonymously, 70 different brands of contraceptive: condoms (500 samples of each of 24 brands, no more than 50 from the same shop), caps, chemicals, safe period calculators, ovulation thermometers, suppositories, foaming tablets and aerosols.

Continued

involves a great deal of arithmetic and more people are helpless with figures than they are with words.

So Tim started off with reports on life insurance, unit trusts, loans for buying a house, premium bonds. He progressed to a Tax-Saving Guide which later appeared every year at the time when the members were filling in their tax return, and led them through it, step by step. *Money Which?* – and particularly the Tax-Saving Guide – was immediately successful and treated respectfully by financial journalists as well as cherished by its members.

Tim was a mainly silent young man who had a gift for absolute concentration, for getting his facts right and for being able to convey them, however complicated they were, in a way that almost anyone could understand. You might say that these are rare gifts, as indeed they are, even taken separately. In combination, very rare indeed.

One of Tim's checkers was a Wing Commander who lived somewhere in Suffolk. Whenever Tim wrote a report – on television sets, loudspeakers, contraceptives, insurance or second mortgages – he sent a draft to the Wing Commander, waiting for the day when the subject would be one on which he was not exceptionally well-informed. The day didn't arrive. Tim often invited him to London so that he might meet this wide-knowledged person and try to thank him, but he never came.

User test: for the report on toy wheelbarrows in *Which?* November 1963.

User test: for the report on sailing dinghies in *Which?* January 1965.

above left: Michael Rubinstein, our libel man, in 1960.

above right: Michael Dunne, research manager of RICA, in 1966.

left: Alastair Macgeorge and Peter Goldman, at the opening of the Consumer Advice Centre in Rushmore, in 1978.

above: Peter Sand, then a project officer, trying out one of the garden cultivators being tested for a report in *Which?* February 1965.

right: Jack Davey, Council member, posing (with son) for the cover photograph of *Which?* November 1959 featuring a report on electric drills.

above: The now famous Bethnal Green garage 'being lovingly converted' in 1957.

right: No. 14 Buckingham Street, CA's London office since 1962.

14

A new director

By then, Caspar Brook had left. The immediate reason was that Caspar, as director, decided that the economical and efficient thing for CA to do was to move out to Harlow, where rents were lower than in London, where there was more space, and which was nearer to the subscription department in Hertford and the Car Test Unit in Gosfield. The London staff refused to go, the majority of the Council sided with the staff and Caspar resigned. In fact, restless, innovative, energetic, he would probably not have stayed much longer – more the type to start something fresh than stay around with a success. As *Which?* was by that time, largely owing to him.

The new director, Peter Goldman, CBE, historian from Cambridge, more recently head of the Conservative Political Centre, friend and colleague of R. A. Butler, was in most ways a very different sort of person from Caspar Brook. The Council obviously required two essentials from a director, old or new — intelligence and integrity. Peter, in addition, was reflective, intellectually most able, publicly impressive, and Conservative. This last was important.

Shortly afterwards, Michael Young handed over the chairmanship to Jennifer Jenkins, wife of Roy Jenkins, at that time Labour's Minister of Aviation, later Chancellor of the Exchequer. Jennifer had a perfectly good non-political career of her own and party politics played at no time any part in CA and certainly not in *Which?*. But the Council was aware that many of its members had at least begun with Labour party sympathies and James Douglas, head of the Conservative Research Centre, was a valuable exception. So, from the beginning, they had included one Conservative and one Labour MP on the Council. Now, with Peter Goldman as director and Jennifer as chairman they must have felt that CA's public face was as politically neutral as its private mind.

Michael had been a relaxed chairman, allowing Council meetings (always held in the evenings because the members had jobs) to go on till ten or later, which suited some people and not others. Anthony Crosland, statutory Labour MP and friend of Michael Young, tended to read the *Evening Standard* when the proceedings bored him, which was often, but most of the others were passionately involved. Jennifer kept the passion within bounds, ending the meetings at nine or even half-past eight, while allowing Paul Fletcher to argue for spending at least 5 per cent of CA's income on campaigning for consumer legislation; Mary Adams to criticise the last *Which?* cover; Jack Davey to doubt whether the reports in *Which?* were as accurate as they used to be; John Thirlwell to question a decision on the grounds that it conflicted with another made five years ago and explicitly reported in the minutes; Rachel Waterhouse, from Birmingham, to point out that not all important events took place in London; and Tony Dumont to press for more interest in consumer organisations overseas.

From *Which?* November 1965 page 348: *At Consumers' Association we were delighted to see Michael Young appointed first Chairman of the Social Science Research Council. But our faces dropped when he told us that his new responsibilities would weigh too heavy to be combined with continued chairmanship of CA. Surely we weren't to lose the man whose inventive intellect and drive had brought CA into existence and stimulated its work for eight years? Happily the Council have found an appropriate way to avoid this and at the same time to say 'thank you'. They have invited Dr. Young to become CA's first President, and his nomination is to be confirmed at a General Meeting to be held shortly.*

Foreign affairs

There had never, in fact, been any lack of such interest. CA, after all, could scarcely have started without help from the American Consumers Union, and *Which?* still learnt from its test methods. Caspar Brook, whose mother was Dutch, had joined with Elisabeth Schadee, Chairman of the Dutch organisation, to form the International Organization of Consumer Unions (IOCU) in 1960, and Paul Fletcher, Tony Dumont and John Thirlwell had been his chief supporters on the Council. Peter Goldman inherited this interest and built on it.

IOCU

This is not the story of IOCU and I mention it here only for its importance to CA and for CA's importance to it.

CA, in founding IOCU with the Dutch consumer organisation, had the help of the Americans, the Belgians and the Australians. All of these have been important to the international organisation which, with member organisations in 37 countries, is notably successful.

Most of the organisations are poor and CA's first contribution to the international body was literally that – its financial contribution. CA's income (though much less than the Americans') was comparatively large and the fractional per cent of it which CA paid annually was an important part of IOCU's funds.

Peter Goldman was CA's second contribution. He could draft a constitution which would not come unstuck. He could make an impressive and moving speech to an audience of any nationality, in either hemisphere. He began by believing in the international idea and stayed with that belief.

The third was the enthusiasm for IOCU of a small number of the staff and a small number of the Council. The number had to be small. Most of the staff considered themselves (with reason) overworked already and had no energy to spare for dealing with requests for information from Malaysia or the Caribbean. Most of the Council members spent enough of their spare time already on CA's home affairs and had no time to spare for conferences in Stockholm or The Hague. But of the staff, the editor (who was also the research director) joined the Technical Director of Consumers Union, Morris Kaplan, in organising international tests (on watches, for instance) while Daphne Grose quietly became an international authority on food. On the Council, Alma Williams, John Thirlwell, Tony Dumont and Paul Fletcher fought obstinately for IOCU, from a background of knowing the people in the overseas organisations and having become friends with them, in Israel or Greece or Singapore.

Consumer organisations in the original six Common Market countries – France, Germany, Italy, Belgium, Luxembourg and The Netherlands – belonged to IOCU, but decided also to form a European consumer organisation — BEUC (Bureau Europeén des Unions de Consommateurs). CA could not be a member, since the UK did not then belong to the Community, but CA was invited, from courtesy, to be an observer at their meetings, and the editor went along to take part in combined tests. BEUC's interests, however, were not, primarily, in testing but in being a pressure group, to put the consumer's case to the Community authorities, and CA had to wait until 1973, when Britain joined the Community, to play its part – which would be considerable – in BEUC's activities.

Soon after Britain joined the Community, Rosemary McRobert persuaded CA to provide the secretariat for a group of British organisations (not only of consumers) interested in, and consulted by government on, the consumer aspects of EEC legislation

They included, for instance, the National Federation of Women's Institutes and the National Federation of Townswomen's Guilds. This now forms the Consumers in the European Community Group (CECG), produces first class reports and opinions on European consumer subjects (such as the Common Agricultural Policy, origin marking of textiles, product liability and so on), is much respected at home – and in Europe where it is the only organisation of its kind.

BEUC

Until 1973, BEUC's activities – as it would be the first to admit – had been muted. The organisations which composed it did not have a large income, few did comparative testing. Some had very little more than goodwill to contribute to a European organisation. BEUC had no staff, no office and no telephone number.

CA was a testing organisation and had a comparatively large income and some staff time to spare. To add to their goodwill, they sent their ex-editor (then deputy director) to work as part-time director for BEUC in Brussels, and with CA's subscription and encouragement, BEUC got its office, its telephone number and a staff of 1½.

There was nothing political in CA's enthusiasm for BEUC. Its motive was practical. Europe was very much of a common market, as far as consumer goods and consumer concerns were concerned. BEUC's job was to impress on the EEC Commission that consumers must be listened to and their interests taken into account when EEC legislation was being drafted. CA had the same job, with its own government, and felt that its hand could only be strengthened by partnership with the organisations of eight other countries. And it was giving support, as well as getting it, which was a good thing.

The Treaty of Rome, which is the Ten Commandments of the European Community, mentions consumers only four times, in passing. When the Community talked about the social partners it meant manufacturers and workers, who between them produce consumer goods, and took no account of the people who bought the goods and without whom the social partners would have nothing to live on. To some extent, this was understandable. When the Treaty of Rome was drawn up, in 1957, consumer organisations were virtually unknown. *Which?* had not started, the concept of consumers and their rights and interests hardly existed. Europe had to learn a new idea and the task of teaching fell largely to BEUC and the organisations that composed it.

The first advance came when the Commission set up a new division, inside its own structure, to concern itself with the matters of the environment and consumer affairs, appointed a Consumer Consultative Committee to advise it, and produced a preliminary Consumer Programme which – from the consumer's point of view – could scarcely be faulted. The programme accepted the rights of consumers to be sold only safe goods; to get compensation legally if goods were faulty; to have all the information and education necessary if they were not to be at a disadvantage when faced by the purveyors of goods or providers of services in the open market; and the right to have their voice heard when governments or others make decisions which affect them economically. To CA and the other organisations these were rights so basic as to scarcely need stating. To the representatives of member governments (who discuss and approve proposals from the Commission before they actually go to the Council of Ministers) they seemed so revolutionary it took over 20 separate meetings to approve them, and only did so finally on condition that a quotation from Adam Smith – who can't be much of a danger since he has been dead for 200 years – should be jettisoned.

History since then has been of the Commission, strongly supported by BEUC, and by the European Parliament and the Economic and Social Committee, attempting to get the promises of the programme put into practice in the form of community legislation. So far, some safety directives have been passed, and there is a European law on food labelling which gives consumers really all they want to know about what tinned and packaged food actually consists of. But draft legislation on product liability (which would enable victims of faulty goods to get compensation without having to prove the manufacturer negligent, which is normally difficult, expensive or impossible) is still draft legislation. So are the directives on misleading advertising and on noise and energy labelling and toy safety and consumer credit. BEUC, which now has a full-time director, British, energetic and able, and a small but adequate staff, soldiers on, supporting and putting pressure on the Commission.

Action Kit: importing a car

BEUC and CA have had one resounding success together. A BEUC survey found that people paid very different prices for cars, according to whether they bought them in one Common Market country or another. For example, the price paid for a basic Ford Escort in the UK was 35% higher than the price paid in Belgium, and 50% higher than that paid in Denmark. Since all three countries are members of a Common Market, this seemed absurd, and Sue Leggate, special projects editor who had been the editor of both *Motoring Which?* and *Holiday Which?* wrote an Action Kit for people who might like to go through the process of buying their car in Europe and saving up to 50% of its purchase price – nearly £1,000 for instance on the basic Ford Escort. CA expected a few hundred requests for this Action Kit and got 42,000.

The success grew. It was quite possible that the British government, pressed by the car industry, would put some obstacle in the way of this private enterprise. At least 2,000 people followed the Action Kit's suggestion and wrote to the government, who did not weaken on the principle of competition. This was then followed by an order from the EEC Commission again supporting the free movement of cars, for the consumers' benefit. Eventually, the European car market must be as common in practice as it is in theory. In the meantime, many motorists have benefited considerably, in the traditional *Which?* way, by saving themselves a lot of money.

ACTION NOW

In this Action Kit we give you some detailed guidelines if you want to try to import a new car yourself from an EEC country. But the Government is reported to be thinking of changing the rules to make it more difficult or even impossible to bring in a car yourself. What can consumers do to stop it?

We've already written to the Minister for Consumer Affairs asking her to resist the pressure to close what is misleadingly called a 'loophole'. But we know from past experience that what really counts is letters from individuals - and the more the better. So, in this section of the Kit, we tell you how to have <u>your</u> say and join in our campaign.

Please write <u>now</u> to:

The Rt.Hon. Sally Oppenheim, M.P.
Minister for Consumer Affairs
House of Commons
London SW1

Tell her:

- that you have read about the big differences in European net car prices and how the car makers charge more for cars in Britain than in any other EEC country
- that you think it unreasonable that British car buyers should have to pay so much more for their cars - even British cars - than consumers in the rest of Europe
- that it would be unfair and quite contrary to the spirit of the Common Market to try and prevent personal imports.

Ask her, too:

- why she thinks people in Britain should have to pay more for cars than other EEC consumers?
- what she intends to do in order to stop any moves to prevent British consumers shopping around for cars in other EEC countries?

Some other points to note:

- send a copy of your letter to your MP (if you don't know your MP's name, ask at your local library) - and tell Mrs Oppenheim that you've done this
- send a copy to your Member of the European Parliament (MEP) - again, your library should be able to tell you his/her name. If they can't, the European Parliament office in London (2 Queen Anne's Gate, London SW1, Tel: 01-222 0411) will tell you. They can also forward your letter to your MEP
- finally, let us know what reaction you get. This will help us plan further campaigns. And even if, having worked through this Action Kit, you are daunted by the idea of importing a car yourself, <u>please</u> do still write to Mrs Oppenheim.

Sue Leggate

Sue Leggate
<u>Editor - Motoring Which?</u>
1st November 1981

Which? January 1962 being collated at Shenval Press. The people standing are, *left to right*, Joan Meier, Dick Nutt, Fred Atterwill, Eirlys Roberts, James Shand, Philip Barbour, A. N. Other, Caspar Brook.

Hertford: the printers and the subscription department

No editors can ever possibly have been luckier than *Which?* was in its printers. James Shand, head of the firm, a Scot, was a distinguished typographer who must have got very little joy out of printing the utilitarian *Which?*, but never said so – just kept editors and verifiers supplied with food and drink until dawn, if necessary, while they made incomprehensible corrections to galley and page proofs. Fred Atterwill, head of the printing shop, would sometimes pass on his printers' edged comments about washing machines which appeared to hold 8½ lb of washing on Thursday afternoon and 9¼ lb on Friday morning. But neither he nor they questioned the need to get it right.

'Hertford'

The mechanics of dealing with members' subscriptions had to be as efficient as the service of information through the magazine: how could one criticise inefficient manufacturers unless one was efficient oneself? So Caspar Brook and Philip Barbour set up a subscription department in Hertford, and enrolled Mary Gaudin, and later Jack Backhouse and Alf Payne who was employed by the printers. It started off in an outhouse of our printers, Simson Shand, in Hertford, moved to an ex-laundry and then to a site on Caxton Hill, presumably reluctant to break the printing link altogether. Hertford was a good economic choice: there were plenty of married women who wanted a job and liked the idea of working for *Which?*. From a management point of view it was a good decision, and no doubt most of the Hertford staff much preferred their country town to London. But Hertford is over 30 miles from London and the London staff missed something in the separation.

The subscription department at Hertford used the same basic system for 20 years – addressograph plates embossed with the names and addresses of members, and supplemented with paper records and correspondence. Addressed wrappers were printed from the plates, the magazines were despatched from the printers in close cooperation with the Post Office. By and large, the system worked, the main complaints being from members who had their copies delivered after reports about the issue appeared in the press, which they considered unfair.

In 1977 Sue Read became head of the subscription department. She has a degree in physics, took postgraduate studies in operational research and management science, and joined CA as marketing statistics officer in 1972. Hertford had much of the raw material for these statistics, in its lists of members, so she became increasingly involved in Hertford's activities and it was a natural (if not immediately obvious) transition that she should become responsible for it when the change to a computer system was clearly needed.

With the arrival of CA's own computer in 1979, Hertford changed, but not fundamentally. The purpose – of serving members as efficiently as possible – did not change, but the method did. The existing staff, mainly married women, had to get used to handling names and addresses in a computer instead of in a file of plates, and this meant a re-training programme. There were a few redundancies, some people changed from subscription work to the data processing for which Sue had recruited David Ensor to set up a department.

The Hertford staff is now 120 and, because of the increase in computer support, is able to handle more work than before (such as the many more books now sold by CA, and *Gardening from Which?*).

The magazine distribution has also changed. The name and

CA's subscription department staff dealing with members' mail.

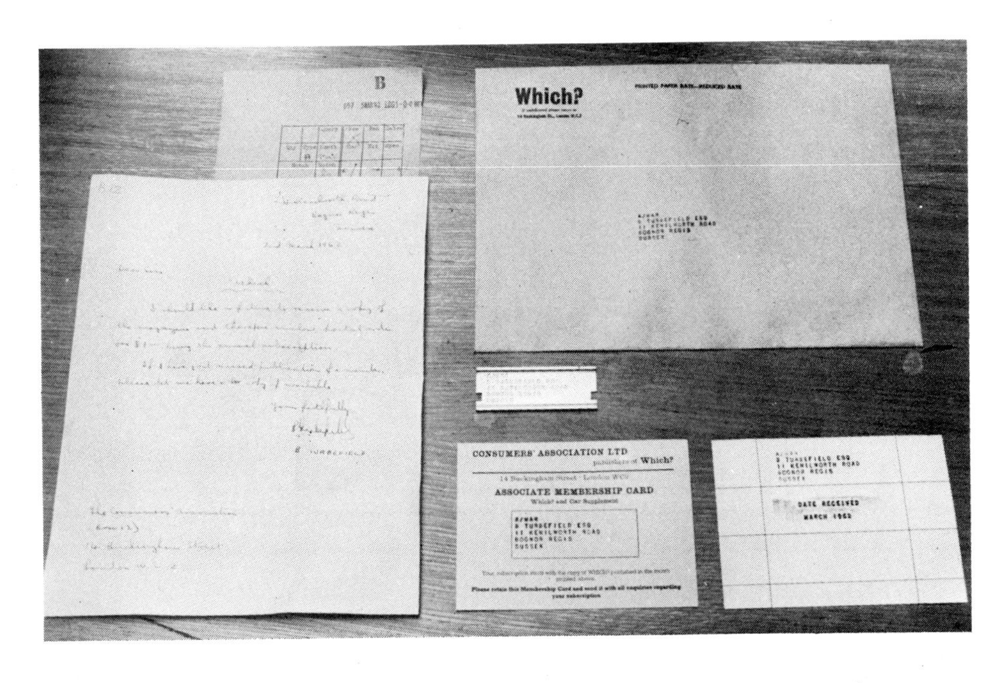

A new member is enrolled, 1962. Methods remained much the same until the computer came in 1979.

address of members are now printed on computer stationery and are then sent to distributors in Bedford, who receive the magazines from the printers in Caerphilly and wrap the copies. On Monday evening, the magazines are all with the Post Office who get them despatched all over the country, to arrive on Thursday. The magazines go by second class post – instead of rebated as previously – and the net result of the new organisation is that members, on the whole, get their copies in time and not after the journalists have reported on them.

The computer was explained to the staff as a sort of filing cabinet from which material can be retrieved fast and easily. This may partly explain Hertford's easy acceptance of the creature. For members, one of its major advantages is the speed with which the staff can look at individual members' records.

In 1981 CA decided to install a computer system in its London HQ – mainly to support and spread CA's research and editorial activities.

Handyman, holiday and *gardening*

Handyman Which? was started as a supplement in November 1971, after a survey which discovered that a sizeable amount of the membership was likely to subscribe to a magazine which would give them test results on do-it-yourself equipment and detailed, *Which?*-type guidance on how to use it. David Holloway, who, exceptionally for a *Which?* project officer, was an engineer, was soon made editor and the circulation is now around 540,000.

Handyman Which? is not for the amateur who is as good as a professional at painting and decorating, putting up shelves, laying a carpet or mending the radio. It is mainly for the thousands of *Which?* members who find themselves owners of houses (and, usually, gardens) which need keeping up and repairing, who have no great experience of being their own handymen, and cannot afford expensive professionals.

In fact, the first person to do any editing of *Handyman Which?* was Maurice Healy, the deputy editor, who attempted to check whether the method suggested in the report on 'How to change a tap washer' actually worked, and rewrote it 5 times. *Handyman Which?* like *Which?* itself and *Money* and *Motoring*, was aimed at the highly intelligent ignoramus, and, succeeding, showed how many of these there were.

Handyman, like *Which?* itself, made a great point of safety – necessarily, because home handymen fall off ladders, use potentially dangerous equipment and have no Factory Acts to protect them. As a result – for example – one unsafe chain saw has been withdrawn by the manufacturer and the BSI is working on a chain saw safety standard.

Holiday Which?

In a way, it could be said that *Which?* embarked on each new supplement reluctantly because it seemed unfair that subscribers to *Which?* itself should be deprived of reports on electric drills or insurance or cars. But in each case it had become obvious that *Which?* did not have enough space to deal in enough detail with cars or money or handywork. So surveys were carried out, to see whether the members would really like, and be prepared to pay for, separate treatment of these subjects.

Holidays were an even more obvious candidate for separate treatment than *Money* or *Motoring*. The surveys suggested a modest interest on the part of the members, and the subscription list began modestly, at around 37,000. It stayed modest for quite a time, began to climb slowly and is now around 250,000.

Holiday Which?'s technique is obviously different from that of the other magazines. You cannot put ten days in Crete in a laboratory and come out with a positive, objective statement about them. But you can get different people to go separately to the same resort or hotel, to report on it without fear of upset advertisers or favour from public relations people. You can check their findings with the past experience of other *Which?* members, and by taking great care, you can give your subscribers a service which is unique in its detachment, and thoroughness, and which they find helpful. Also, it has nice pictures and it's jollier to read about ski resorts or villages in the unspoilt parts of Mallorca than it is about washing machines.

Holiday Which? has been, and is, a campaigner. It started off with an extremely critical report on tour operators, went on to the surcharges which hit holidaymakers unexpectedly when they think that everything has been taken into account, and then dealt with air fares. In a capitalist society, theoretically dedicated to the principle of free competition, it seems grossly hypocritical that

left to right: Julian Edwards (senior research manager), Sue Leggate (special projects editor) and Chris Gill (editor, *Holiday Which?*) at CA's silver jubilee garden party, July 1982.

European airlines should be able to join in a cartel (IATA) which keeps air fares exactly where it wants them – high. It seems hypocritical and it is, and *Holiday Which?* has joined with other consumer organisations in the EEC in the attempt to break the cartel. The British government, one might say, has a fairly liberal attitude on air fares, but on the whole, the campaign has still some way to go.

Thirty seven percent of *Which?* members take their holidays in the UK, 21% in France and 10% in Greece. The most popular report of all has been that on Crete. I do not know whether the independence that *Holiday Which?* makes possible is its most important achievement, or the one its subscribers value most. With a *Holiday Which?* report on the choice of cheap tickets, and its assessment of hotels, you can now plan your own holiday, without benefit of tour operators, and without overspending. Many of our members value that return to adventure, and to the casual ingredient in the true holiday.

One of the *Holiday Which?* inspectors asked at the tourist office in Tenerife for the current bus timetable. There wasn't one. "Oh why?" asked the inspector, "You had one last year". "Yes", said the clerk, "we did, but there was a mistake of 1 hour in the departure time of one bus. A German holidaymaker wrote to the Tourism Ministry and complained. What does one hour matter, waiting for a bus on holiday in the sun? This year we just decided not to produce *any* timetable.

Gardening from Which?

Gardening from Which? has been launched in CA's silver jubilee year. It grew naturally out of *Handyman Which?* many of whose subscribers said that they would like to see gardening reports in a separate supplement. The editor is Roger Davies, who bought his first packet of seeds when he was seven and edited a Gardening News Sheet somewhere in Lancashire at the age of ten. Then he took a Ph.D in chemistry at Leeds University, joined CA as a project officer and now cultivates a half-acre garden in Staplehurst, apart from editing *Gardening from Which?*. He has an assistant editor and four project officers, of whom one was a tree advisory officer in Suffolk, and one the editor of a tropical weed magazine.

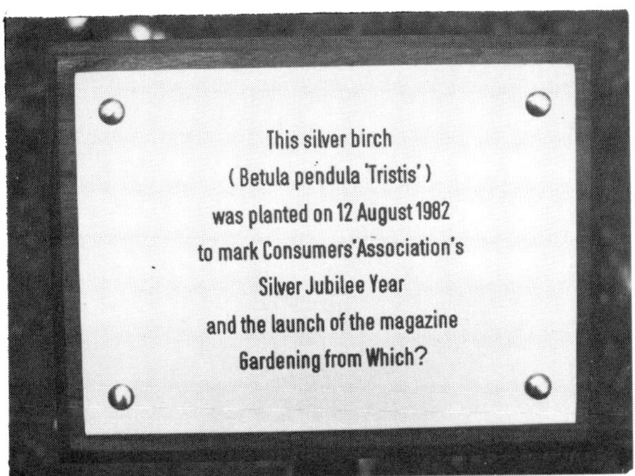

Roger Davies, editor of *Gardening from Which?* with John Thirlwell, founder-Council member, at the launch of *Gardening*, August 1982.

There is something engagingly traditional about the first issue of *Gardening from Which?*. It chooses best buys, one of which is a mail order tulip, little-known, expensive but of outstanding quality. It informs you that the tulip came from Central Asia and the name from the Turkish word for a turban.

It gives a best buy hedgetrimmer and heavily emphasizes electrical safety. It harks back to a 1963 *Which?* report on flower-delivery services and gets beyond them to the possibly wiser alternatives of yellow pages, credit cards and the telephone. It tells you *Which tree?* for a small garden, how most economically to heat a greenhouse, how to live through the year on your own fruit and vegetables and how to use old growing bags. It warns you about tetanus and about any attempt to enter the UK with more than 2 kg of dahlia tubers, and tells you without pity what to do in your garden in August.

There are innumerable gardening books and some gardening magazines which are popular and good. *Gardening from Which?* is fetching to look at (modest-sized full-colour illustrations which do not impinge on the text), intensely practical, forthright, assuming the reader's inexperience, clear and coolly-written. It should suit *Which?* gardeners.

The CA laboratory

In the beginning *Which?* had to use outside laboratories to do its testing, and was lucky to find them, scattered through the countryside and some abroad. Most were private or belonged to specialist organisations, occasionally to local government or universities. They charged very little and showed an astonishing amount of enthusiasm (at least at the beginning of each test) and patience. CA was deeply dependent on these laboratories – any mistake they might make, we were responsible for – and felt warmly for their kindness. CA was very demanding. Sometimes we envied the country peace which surrounded most of them.

But eventually we felt – some more strongly than others – CA had to become independent and have its own lab. We searched for somewhere near and cheap – Thamesmead and by railway sidings in Battersea, discussed the possibilities of Cambridge, and eventually settled on an ex-Beecham lab in Harpenden, because we could just about afford it, it was reasonably near the subscription department in Hertford and the Car Test Unit in Gosfield, and (most important) not too far from the project officers in Buckingham Street. Also – although this was not an argument put forward to CA's Council – it is a most agreeable little town.

There were many things to be said for CA's having its own lab. The staff would be part of CA's staff and so entirely involved with it. The project officers would have complete authority over the lab staff. CA would be able to impose its own standards of accuracy and relevance in the testing.

It could develop its own test-methods. And it could get nearer to the continuous testing of at least the most important pieces of domestic equipment, which had been CA's dream for a long time. Gerald Bailey began by moving towards this continuous testing so that, in between the major reports on products such as vacuum cleaners and washing machines, *Which?* could tell its members about changes in specific brands in *What's New*. Now the lab is testing washing machines continuously, so that the *Which?* reports on them will be up to date (within a month or so) and the same should soon be true of driers and dishwashers.

The danger that some people foresaw was that the lab would get too in-grown and technical, too far away from people's homely needs. I don't think that this has happened. To begin with, Dennis Howard, John and Pat Knightley and Chris Evans came over from the laboratories that *Which?* had long used, bringing with them a very practical tradition. Harpenden can call on a panel of more than 5,000 CA members who carry out user and taste tests in their homes or in the lab in groups of ten or twelve, on anything required and ensure that the final judgement corresponds to what the users know they need, not what the technician thinks they ought to get.

But we also realised that our own lab could not do all the testing we wanted. Food, medical, textile and other specialist projects would still need the help of outside labs, and we still use some of them.

Testing for others

CA is proud of the lab. It now does testing, not only for *Which?* but for government departments, international agencies such as W.H.O., some research organisations and for consumer associations in Europe and the Far East.

These last two are particularly interesting. There is a group of consumer associations in Europe, the European Testing Group, most of them members of BEUC but extending beyond the European Community to countries such as Norway and Sweden.

Domestic science students helping with the tests for a report on detergents in *Which?* September 1959.

The kitchen units (now superseded) for user tests at CA's Harpenden laboratory, in the mid-1970's.

For some products – cameras and hi-fi for instance – most of the brands are sold in most European countries so it makes sense for one organisation to carry out the test for all of them. In practice, of course, it's not quite as simple as that, and the usual result is a few countries joining in one test, and a different few another.

In spite of the difficulties of language, temperament, and national habits, the system works loosely but quite well, and the organisations gain financially by sharing the costs. Peter Sand of CA co-ordinates the tests at the moment and Harpenden does much of the photographic testing and is moving into hi-fi and television.

I don't think it is boasting to point out that the consumer associations of affluent countries (through IOCU) are unselfish in their practical support of consumers in the Third World. Tests on outboard motors for Malaysian fishing boats and water pumps for villages in the Third World may sound a remote kind of help but providing information enabling the fishermen and villagers to get more food and water, more economically, for themselves, is similar to what *Which?* does for its own members.

From CATR's brochure: *There are extensive and adaptable facilities for a wide variety of comparative testing. These include computer-controlled environmental rooms and cabinets with a temperature range from −30°C to +45°C and relative humidity up to 95%, automatic logging of data; optical and photometric equipment for testing photographic and related apparatus; endurance rigs for life tests on electrical, mechanical and hydraulic products.*

The staff at CATR includes people with industrial experience and qualifications in a wide range of disciplines including chemistry, physics, metallurgy, geology, mechanical and electrical engineering, home economics, photography, social sciences, mathematics, statistics, and market research.

Consumers' Association Testing and Research

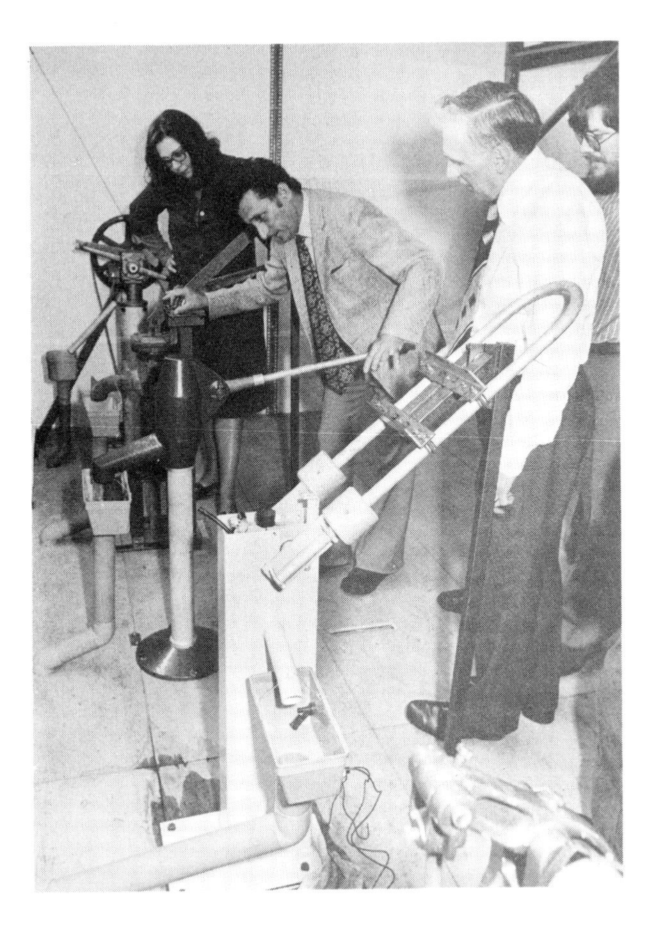

Pumps for use in developing countries being tested at CA's laboratory in 1981.

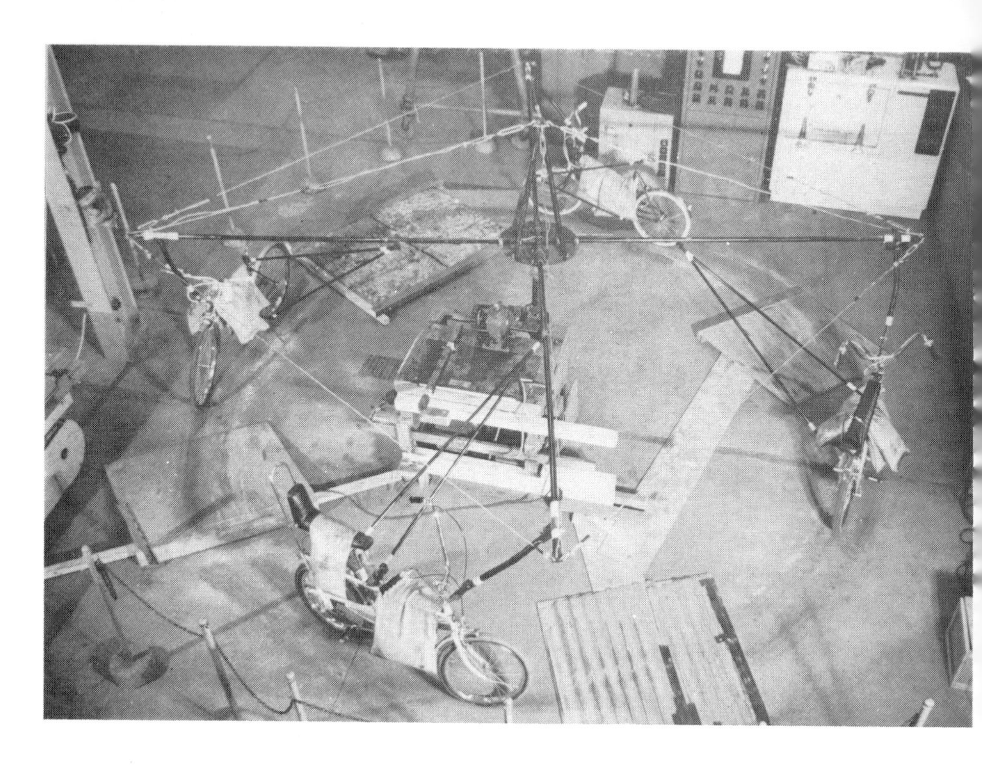

Endurance test, done at CA's Harpenden laboratory, for the small bicyles report in *Which?* 1972.

A user test for the bicyles report in *Which?* May 1975.

Television and books

The press, radio and television had been generous to *Which?* from the beginning, reporting its reports, mentioning it as news. More ambitiously, Mary Adams, a Council member who had been Head of Television Talks at the BBC, persuaded the BBC to produce a series based on *Which?* reports, called 'Choice'. Edith Rudinger was given the job of seeing that *Which?*'s principles were kept intact, all brand names mentioned, and facts and emphases kept exactly as in the *Which?* reports. Everyone applauded the courage of the BBC and the unbendable will of Edith Rudinger; but it was not, to put it mildly, good television. Thereafter CA left the programmes to the professionals, simply providingfacts and other material, and staff or Council members to explain the *Which?* view, as required.

In 1973, CA forged what was to prove a very successful and long-lasting relationship with Thames Television. We began by providing research and information for a programme entitled *Good Afternoon*. This arrangement developed into a series of

---

From CA's evidence to the Molony Committee, paragraph 45: *We strongly recommend that the BBC should be specifically empowered and the ITA required to make provision for programmes giving the results of independently-conducted comparative tests, with brand names and prices of products.*

---

contracts with *Money-Go-Round*. This was a consumer magazine programme also in the afternoon (although days and times during the afternoon varied between series) and was presented by Tony Bastable and Joan Shenton. The programme included coverage of *Which?* reports and featured specially commissioned CA research as well as numerous appearances by CA staff, most notably David Tench. Through *Money-Go-Round*, CA was able to reach a much wider audience than through *Which?*; about 5 million people watched *Money-Go-Round* each week.

The last series of *Money-Go-Round* came to an end in March 1982. However CA has maintained its close relationship with Thames Television and with *Money-Go-Round*'s Producer, Mary McAnally. We are now looking forward to having a large input to the new series of consumer programmes which Mary and Thames will produce and which will be shown on Channel 4 beginning in November 1982.

Books

Edith Rudinger, who had emerged from the early BBC adventure with personal credit, soon found another. She had already had a varied career in CA – joined as its Secretary, helped to choose the first director, instituted the system of coding advertisements so

---

From CA's Annual Report for the year ended 31 March 1964: Choice, *the monthly BBC television programme that consisted entirely of 'reports on reports' based on* Which?, *continued into the financial year 1963/64. The April 1963 programme, which dealt with carpets, was considered to be among the best of the* Choice *series. The particular series concluded with the May 1963 programme, based on two topical* Which? *reports.*

Negotiations for the next series of Choice *programmes were started in the summer, but the new – in content slightly different – series, which will be an uninterrupted, not just a six-monthly one, was not restarted until April 1964.*

The fortnightly five-minute BBC sound programmes, based on Which? *reports, continued without a break until October 1963.*

CA's ad hoc participation in sound, BBC television and independent companies' television programmes continued throughout the year.

---

that only the profitable ones were continued, became chief correspondent (organising the answering of members' letters) and then press officer. Then she started, almost by accident, on her most successful stage yet: the *Consumer Publications.*

Which? discovered a large amount of provable facts about goods and services and set them out in such a way that the readers could be sure of making, if they wanted to, a sensible choice and of using their money intelligently. This was what the thousands of members wanted, and they all wanted the same thing.

But at any one time, there are always people who have a special problem, which concerns only a few of them. Testing would not solve it, and guidance that was going to be any use would have to be set out at length, taking far more space than *Which?* could afford.

One example of these problems was anything to do with consumer law. If you see something in a shop window that you like, marked £10 (which you can afford), ask for it inside and are told that the ticket was wrongly marked, it's £20 (which you can't afford), can you demand to be sold whatever it is for £10? If someone comes and makes you an offer for your house, you spend time and money on arrangements for buying another and the offer is withdrawn at the last moment, can you get any redress? If you asked a shop assistant whether a blouse was made of cotton, he said "Yes" and you found when you washed it at the right temperature for cotton – hot – that it was made of viscose (rayon), would you get your money back? (I use the past tense here, because since the Textile Products Regulations in 1974, the fibre content must be shown on the label.) However, the story

---

From CA's Annual Report for the year ended 31 March 1973: *The Special Projects Unit continued to research monthly features for sale to the mass-circulation* Daily Mirror *and conducted investigations for a London evening newspaper, local radio stations and independent television. An agreement was recently made to supply material on a regular basis to the ITV consumer programme* Good Afternoon.

---

began in 1960, when a book by a lawyer, Aubrey Diamond, and an economist, Harvey Cole, *The Consumer and the Law* answered many of these questions, which needed answering. But it was out of print in 1962.

Caspar Brook had suggested to Edith that CA might produce one. She found a lawyer, David Tench, who worked in Inland Revenue and had time to spare in the evenings and at weekends. Between them, they produced *The law for consumers* which was instantly successful and led to a long series of Consumer Publications – some even more successful.

Basically, the series set out to deal with problems – *On getting divorced, What to do when someone dies, Avoiding back trouble, Getting a new job*. They were daughters – or, if you like, daughters-in-law – of *Which?* in that they followed a family tradition of being based on exceptionally hard work, rigorous verifying, and insistence that every sentence should be understandable, by anyone. Considering that the information they had to communicate was in many cases to do with medicine or English law, this was an achievement of which Edith (philosophy at St. Andrews), Anne Morris (Anglo-Saxon at Bristol) and David Tench (lawyer) could be proud, if they were complacent, as they are not.

In November 1977 Anthony Land was appointed CA's Head of Publishing and production of books has increased steadily since then. The books which aim to provide well presented information that will help readers in their everyday lives are sold not only direct to CA members but also to the public in book shops through CA's arrangement with the publishers Hodder & Stoughton. In CA's top ten best sellers are the *Which? Book of Money* ('everything you always wanted to know about money – if you had known who to ask!') and the *Which? Book of Do-it-yourself*, produced with the help of the *Money Which?* and *Handyman Which?* staff respectively.

From CA's Annual Report for the year ended 31 March 1980: *For the second year running, CA's sales from book publishing increased by more than 50 per cent to reach a record £700,000.*

left: The first consumer law book was published by the Co-operative Union in 1960.

left: The first of the Consumer Publications, *The Law for Consumers*, was published in 1962.

above: David Tench, who wrote it.

The *Good Food Guide*

No one would suggest that *Which?* and the *Good Food Guide* were, in any sense, relations, but they became partners when both were quite young.

Raymond Postgate, who started the *Good Food Guide*, was the son of Postgate's Latin Grammar. The only language allowed at Sunday lunch, when he was a child, was Latin, and, if he or his sister made a grammatical mistake when they asked for more Yorkshire pudding – Raymond told me – they didn't get it. This background can scarcely have been responsible for the fact that he was a believing and practising socialist, a connoisseur of wine and food, but it must have had something to do with the Augustan periods in which he wrote. He and his wife Daisy, troubled by the low standards of British restaurant cooking, founded the Good Food Club, long before *Which?* was thought of, collecting the verdicts of people throughout the country on named restaurants. Raymond wrote his own summaries of their opinions and the result was published as the *Good Food Guide*. It was the first British guide to good restaurants and the members of the Good Food Club certainly bought it for its usefulness; they also enjoyed the richness of its prose.

In 1962 CA took over the publishing of the *Good Food Guide*, while Raymond continued as Editor. This made financial sense for the Guide (Raymond was not a business man) and also, eventually, for CA. And they had much in common in spirit. The Guide named restaurants, as CA named products, and neither minced words when it came to saying what they thought of either. Both refused all advertising, and bought and paid for products or meals anonymously, and neither had finance outside their members' payments. Both had started with the aim of raising standards in the area in which they dealt (goods and services, and restaurant food). Both were valued by their readers for their practical usefulness.

But they never pretended to think with one mind. Raymond was quietly contemptuous of washing machines and dish-washers. Most *Which?* project officers neither knew the difference between a Barsac and a Rudesheimer nor would have thought the difference important if they had known. And, although they acknowledged that, if ten people thought a restaurant good and none thought it bad, this constituted a fact, they were uneasy with what appeared to be subjective opinions when they were used to dealing with what could be tested objectively. It was noticeable, however, that they used the Guide for reference if they wanted to eat out in style.

When Raymond Postgate retired Christopher Driver took over as editor. He was a friend and admirer of Raymond's, much younger, a classical scholar, with a highly polished silver Latin style to succeed Raymond's gold. During the next twelve years the reputation of the Guide was maintained by him and by his strictly anonymous chief inspector, and by all the members of the Good Food Club who went through the tedious business of filling in forms noting the price and quality of the *sole normande* or the vichyssoise, passing judgment on the service, condemning Muzak. Other food guides appeared, and were successful, but none had the puritanical independence, and therefore, I believe, the authority of the *Good Food Guide*.

There is no doubt whatever that the *Good Food Guide* helped to raise the standard of cooking in this country's restaurants. Some would say that it was crucial in doing so, and that in the process it has helped the British tourist industry. What it has certainly done is to give its users a great deal of happiness, on the one hand, by telling them where they can get a good meal, and saved them much misery, on the other, by guiding them away from where they would have got a bad one.

In 1979, CA took over *Drinkers' Digest* which provides topical assessments of wine, turned it into the *Which? Wine Monthly* and since 1981 the annual *Which? Wine Guide* complements the *Good Food Guide*.

Research Institute for Consumer Affairs

Michael Dunne came to CA, as a project officer, very early on, an engineer from de Havilland's. It seemed strange to the editor, but not to Michael, that the projects he enjoyed most were concerned more with people than with machinery – testing life-jackets with the help of volunteers in the Admiralty's swimming club in Bath, nylons with students in teachers' training colleges, children's shoes in schools in Ealing, the operation of one-man buses in London. This was not testing goods in a laboratory or by asking people what they thought of them, but by observing how people used them. It was experience he needed when he became research manager of RICA.

The Research Institute for Consumer Affairs was started by Michael Young, when *Which?* was beginning to be successul. Michael Young thought that *Which?* could be left to look after the interests of the individual shopper, faced with a choice among goods and commercial services. He wanted now to do something for consumers faced with no choice – vis à vis private monopolies, public services, and the nationalised industries. CA, in those days, could not ask its members to contribute

---

From CA's Annual Report for the year ended 31 March 1964: *As a charitable trust, RICA qualifies, unlike CA, for grants from foundations and other sources for specific pieces of research. It retains exclusive editorial control over all published material based on supported research.*

---

financially to this kind of research. So Michael set up RICA, a charitable sister organisation to CA, to do the job, so that the research could be paid for from charitable funds.

Early essays

RICA started off, under the direction of Brian Groombridge, to investigate these services and produced a series of what were called *essays & enquiries* on subjects including, for example, *London Stations, Town Planning, General Practice, Fair Trading* (which mainly celebrated the passing of the Weights and Measures Act 1963), *Estate Agents, British Co-operatives,* and *Elderly Consumers.*

In general, they used experts in the subjects chosen, and supplemented their information by small surveys among CA members or carried out by members of CA or of consumer groups. The studies came to tentative conclusions and sometimes included blueprints for improvements. *London Stations,* for instance, put teams of observers (one man and one woman) in seven-hour shifts on to the London termini and registered their observations. They found the trains punctual, waiting rooms uninviting, lavatories patchy, food in refreshment rooms 'standard', information services criticizable and the most noticeable concession to non-English speaking visitors: *Bureau de Change.* The essay concluded with an entirely different vision of the future, in which stations would become 'popular places to linger in . . . a place to enjoy a coffee at all times of day and night, a place to take your girlfriend on a wet afternoon.'

From *New Nations,* page 46: *Opportunities exist for consumers in Western countries to help their counterparts in the developing world. It would be dangerous if the Western example encouraged aspirations which cannot be fulfilled in the foreseeable future. Equally, against a background of increasing authoritarianism, it is useful for governments in the developing world to be reminded of the needs of their people, consumers in the widest sense. The encouragement of voluntary efforts to improve living standards, preferably in the context of community action, could help to ensure that development will be responsive to the needs of the people.*

One of the *essays & enquiries* was on *New Nations*, which was effectively about consumers in the Third World; at that time, 1964, the phrase was not freely used. In the introduction, the authors said 'The modern consumer movement as we know it is essentially a product of post-industrial societies with developed economies and liberal-democratic institutions. Underdeveloped countries, by definition, are only just embarking on industrialisation. In many cases they have authoritarian regimes. Under these circumstances it would be curious if consumer protection took the same forms in the new nations as it has in the affluent West.'

The studies were designed to ask questions and raise issues rather than to offer definitive answers. They pointed the way to research or action that was needed in matters of concern to consumers, for the guidance of both consumers and those who served them.

Elderly Consumers considered the gap left by consumer organisations (which consider consumer needs but not specifically those of elderly consumers) and organisations concerned with the welfare of the elderly (but not specifically their needs as consumers). For this study, the Watford Consumer Group investigated the supply (or rather the lack of supply) of attractive, comfortable shoes for elderly women. Others looked at the difficulties caused by official communications, inconsiderate planning, shortage of small packs of food, high-pressure selling, to people whose income and self-confidence may be getting less while their physical handicaps increase. The study concluded with many recommendations – for preventing hypothermia, for legal improvements in the law on credit, for better official communication, for planning, finance, housing, help on budgeting, better service from retailers, and above all for the kind of self-help which gives the lift to self-confidence that charity often knocks down.

The studies were carried out by a tiny organisation, with very little money, and could not have the weight to stir governments or lead to important follow-up action. But *Which?* followed up *London Stations* and *Estate Agents* and *The Elderly* with its own investigations, and carried the arguments one stage further.

And the compassion which shows in *Elderly Consumers* had its natural consequence in the long series of comparative reports for people with disabilities which Michael Dunne was to produce.

Later projects

An early RICA project, managed by Michael Dunne, was funded by Duncan Guthrie, head of Action for the Crippled Child, and by James Loring, director of the Spastics Society. The idea was to carry out comparative tests on equipment for disabled people as *Which?* carried out comparative tests for able-bodied people. The Car Test Unit tested the three-wheeled trike (which it did not like at all), and, later on, cars converted for the use of disabled people (which it much preferred).

I do not think that RICA would claim to have been a pioneer in work for disabled people. It played its part in society's growing concern for the under-privileged in general, and continued, on the same lines, in other such subjects. An enquiry into heating for the elderly, for example; an investigation into the way in which drugs with dangerous side-effects, from which Western consumers are protected, can be sold unchecked in the third world; and, lately, investigations into simpler official forms, designed to help the less thoroughly educated.

Large cake and a four-colour cover on *Which?*, for the 10th anniversary, October 1967.

CA's members and non-members

I cannot remember who first began to worry about CA's soul – as distinct from survival – and rather think it must have been someone from outside, a journalist perhaps. The press had been on CA's side from the beginning, and would continue to be so, but it cannot allow people to get above themselves, and began to reproach CA with being 'middle class'. Since the staff suspected that the journalists lived in Greenwich and had nannies in the nursery, they sometimes found this hard to take. But CA's habit was to accept criticism and try to find out whether it was justified.

Anyone who talks or writes about class in this country is walking on eggshells. One can get round the danger, to some extent, by using the market research people's socio-economic groupings, A to E, based primarily on occupation, with concessions to social tradition. Thus AB is the highest grouping, including people with the highest incomes, mostly management and the professions, C_1 is white-collar workers, C_2 skilled manual workers, D unskilled workers and E the poor.

Using these groups, CA found – as did all other consumer testing organisations from New York to New Zealand – that a large percentage of its members were A or B, primarily male, aged between 25 and 45, and had stayed at school or university beyond the age of 18. The grouping in the population as a whole is more or less evenly divided between the sexes, with the majority in groups C_1 and C_2, and who left school around 15.

So CA had to accept that most of its members were middle class (if that is the shorthand one wants to use) and no one was impressed by the argument that all revolutions, except that of Spartacus, have been started by the middle class. CA was left with the feeling that its members were already privileged and it should try to spread its usefulness further.

Consumer Groups

The first attempt was the Consumer Groups, started early on by Caspar Brook.

The original idea of the groups was that they should publish magazines reporting on local supplies of goods and services, as *Which?* reported on them nationally, and so bring consumer information nearer to the point at which people were actually paying for the goods and services – filling in the holes left in the national net. There was also certainly the idea that in this way CA was reaching less privileged people – grass roots, they called them, presumably in contrast to the orchid plants in Blackheath and Hampstead.

There is no doubt whatever that the consumer groups give their members useful local information about the prices of goods and the quality of commercial services in their area. They go beyond this, and bring pressure to bear on local authorities to provide better public services, such as playgrounds for children and access to buildings for disabled people.

The Federation of Consumer Groups is recognised by government and international bodies as being able to speak in the consumer interest with the authority of local knowledge. And all this has been achieved by people working voluntarily, on top of their ordinary jobs, expecting, and certainly getting, no reward.

But it is no good pretending that the people who are members of local consumer groups are any different, in income, type of job, or education from the people who subscribe to *Which?*. They may live in a small community and be strongly rooted in local affairs, but they probably subscribe to *Which?* anyway and can no more claim to be typical of the majority than can any other *Which?* subscriber.

CA had to try again if it wanted to enlarge its constituency.

From CA's Annual Report for the year ended March 1963: *Last October I was able to tell you that 14 independent local groups of consumers had established themselves in different parts of the country. Now there are 50 such groups and, in March of this year, the Federation of Consumer Groups was established.*

We believe that the group movement is very important and that the establishment of the Federation of Consumer Groups was a momentous occasion.

It all began with a conference called in October 1961 by Consumers' Association in Aylesbury. This was followed by a second conference last year at Consumers' Association when it was decided in principle that some sort of national organisation should be established. That first time in Aylesbury we invited local Which? *readers to attend, and more than 500 did so. The first local group, in Oxford and district, was formed ten days later. The members of groups are mostly made up of lively young people from a very wide range of professions and occupations. Chairmen of Groups include a housewife, a BOAC pilot, a serving soldier, two University dons, a GP, a medical consultant, an industrial designer, an architect and a quality control engineer.*

These groups already have a heartening vitality. Their main job has been to act as the local counterparts of Which?

From CA's Annual Report for the year ended March 1965: *The number of local consumer groups has grown to 93, of whom 10 receive grants from their local authorities. They are now administered in twelve regions and have a combined membership around 12,000. Magazines are published by 85 groups and are increasingly professional in content and presentation.*

All groups have now investigated some aspect of the public services. Many have achieved victories in the improvement of facilities of mothers and children in hospitals, the reorganisation of refuse collection, the rebuilding or modernisation of public lavatories, and so on. A number of national projects are planned for 1965/66, and the first weekend training conference for group officers will be held at Keele University this September.

From Stores & Shops, June 1965, page 23: *Ever since* Which? *first hesitantly emerged from its earliest home – a Bethnal Green garage – in 1957, people have been saying that it will never really catch on. The pessimists forecast that it would be involved in widespread libel actions, that the combined pressure of manufacturers would prove too strong for it, and that no magazine could conceivably keep its head above water without advertising.*

On all of these counts the critics have been confounded. But there was one charge which was laid against it early in its career which it has never yet overcome – that it circulates largely amongst just the very sort of people who are least in need of its help. Notwithstanding its meteoric circulation which has now reached a peak of 450,000 and a readership, presumably, of several times that number, yet these people continue to be of the 'educated' class – for lack of a better word – middle-class professional people and their families. This has always been Which?*'s greatest obstacle: how to present its copiously-documented, intensely-reasoned and carefully balanced judgements in a readable form to the vast mass of the* Daily Mirror*-reading public whose judgement in matters of consumer protection is most in need of tuition.*

The new Director of Consumers' Association, Mr. Peter Goldman, now seems to have found a solution. This new teaching is not in fact to be done through Which?*, but through country-wide 'consumer clinics', which will give advice to housewives before they go shopping. At some future stage of the plan it is hoped to enlist Government help in providing finance. In Mr. Goldman's opinion, "if you are going to break through the class barrier you can't do it through publications. You can do it through broadcasting, perhaps through the press, but above all, through consumer clinics".*

Of Which?*'s readership, only 30 per cent are lower middle class or skilled working class; the unskilled working class are hardly touched at all. But with this new scheme, the ordinary housewife may now visit a 'clinic' to get advice on a refrigerator – on size and prices, on 'best buys'.*

Consumer Advice Centres

Soon afterwards, CA's Council decided that one way to do this might be to produce a popular edition of *Which?*, something like the *Daily Mirror*. The editor took part in collecting people from the street and discussing *Which?* with them. Once, in Hackney, a young woman, clearly intelligent, told her that the magazine might be written in Greek for all she could understand of it; and an older man explained the extreme care with which he had chosen a washing machine for his wife, consulting a series of relations and friends and shop assistants.

Reading matter, at whatever level, was not the way to get consumer information to a wider public. The Council abandoned the idea of a popular *Which?*. An impression remained that perhaps many people like to get their information not by reading but by word of mouth.

By this time, the Austrian consumers' organisation had set up in Vienna a Consumer Centre where people could look at, handle, and thoroughly investigate goods they intended to buy, discuss them with the staff and get honest information and advice about what to buy, through conversation. In Germany there were similar advice centres in the main cities of the German *Länder*. Peter Goldman found out about the Austrian centre when visiting Vienna on IOCU business and came back convinced that this was a possible way of enlarging CA's constituency. Here was a means of getting tested information to people who were not prepared to read test reports but who would listen to a friendly person speaking with the authority of the reports and applying the information to their specific problem.

Having the conviction was one thing, putting it into practice was another. The Austrians had special grants and the Germans had federal and central government subsidies for their advice centres. CA had only the money provided by its members and they provided it in order to get the magazine, with its expensive test reports and increasingly expensive paper, printing and postage. There was not much left over when all the bills were paid.

However, the Council never forgot the "middle class" reproach and Peter Goldman was able eventually to persuade them that Advice Centres might be a way of breaking the middle class barrier and that the necessary money should be spent on an experimental advice centre.

The consumer advice centre in Kentish Town, North London, was to run for over two years and deal with other 40,000 enquiries. What helped was that it was in a main shopping street, in a converted shop. It provided factual and impartial information, free, to all comers who wanted advice before buying. This advice centre was an experimental project and by 1971 it was clear that it was a highly successful experiment – more successful than the Council (though perhaps not the Director) had expected. It had assimilated a lot of experience and data, which enabled CA to build up the information system and training that any future centres would need. Above all, it proved to be the spark for one of the most rapid developments in local government services.

Following the Kentish Town success, CA launched a campaign to persuade local authorities to establish similar consumer advice centres. CA had felt justified in paying for the experiment, but could not have paid for centres all over the country. CA had

---

From CA's Annual Report for the year ended March 1969: *A temporary* Which? *Advice Centre in Croydon – well received by shoppers and by the local authority, traders and press – has given CA valuable experience in translating the 'consumer clinic' idea into British terms. It is to be followed during the next year by other pilot centres, at which the range of subjects dealt with and the duration of the experiment can be progressively extended.*

From CA's Annual Report for the year ended March 1970: *In 1969 this was piloted for short periods on temporarily rented sites. In 1970 a fully-fledged Centre is operating in properly equipped premises well situated – at 242 Kentish Town Road – in a principal north London shopping area. It offers free advice on an expanding range of consumer goods, and is proving increasingly successful both in reaching the less socially privileged and in building up research information. Next year we intend to seek local authority and other sponsorship for some of the ideas the Centre embodies.*

Getting advice about buying a washing machine . . . . . . so that it will fit the space in the kitchen.

proved the need for such centres and established that they had to be operated like a shop, in an informal atmosphere, and had to be in a shopping site where people could find them easily. The centres were to give general consumer information, pre-shopping counselling and help with post-shopping complaints. In other words, a complete and professional consumer advice service was, for the first time in the UK, to be offered to anyone who needed it.

Only one year later, in 1972, the first local authority consumer advice centre opened and by September 1972 there were five. One of them, in the borough of Havering, in East London, was staffed and managed by CA on behalf of the local authority. This gave CA the opportunity to develop the service further and to set up a special advice centre service unit (ACSU). Havering was to

---

From paragraph 32 of the White Paper 'The Attack on Inflation' (Cmnd 6151): *The Government propose to finance through a special Exchequer grant more consumer advice centres in local authority areas to assist consumers who have complaints or queries about particular retail prices in their district. There are now 60 centres, there will be 80 by the end of 1975, and the Government will discuss a plan to open many more by the end of 1976 with the local authorities. The Government will encourage more work on local price comparisons indicating best value for money, and will accelerate the programme of price display and unit pricing.*

From the Department of Prices and Consumer Protection Circular No. 9/75 of September 1975: *Consumers' Association pioneered the introduction in the United Kingdom of consumer advice centres offering a comprehensive consumer advice service and has been closely involved in their subsequent development. It is therefore particularly well placed to advise on all aspects of the establishment and organisation of such centres, and has developed information services and training programmes specifically to meet their needs. The Department understands that Consumers' Association is prepared, within the limits of its available resources, to provide specialist advice and consultancy services to those authorities considering setting up a consumer advice centre. Authorities wishing to discuss these services should contact the Advice Centre Servicing Unit at Consumers' Association, and* not *the Department.*

---

prove a great success both in its own right and as a model for other local authorities to copy. In November 1973, the then Minister for Trade and Consumer Affairs, Sir Geoffrey Howe, held a series of meetings with local authorities, encouraging them to develop local consumer advice centres.

The local authority reorganisation in 1974 was the turning point. Consumers' Association, via ACSU, organised endless visits from newly-elected local politicians to see Havering and other centres. The number of new centes began to grow – to 110 in December 1976 and around 125 in May 1977. The Government announced that it would pay some 3 million pounds towards the running costs of consumer advice centres throughout the UK. CA's initiatives had certainly brought results and had temporarily changed the face of consumer protection in the UK, making the development of consumer advisory services a fundamental part of 99% of all local authority consumer protection services.

During the summer of 1982, some of the advice centres that had been closed by the removal of grants from centres since 1978, have started to open again.

The Advice Centres were a courageous experiment. As a public service, they are a success. They are a step towards CA's goal of penetrating deep into the population. There's still a long walk ahead.

Market Intelligence Unit

Rebecca Wolf applied for the job of Market Intelligence Officer in 1963, out of curiosity, and the Editor almost turned her down, thinking she talked too fast. But *Which?* was being criticised for testing too few of the available brands and for seeming not to know enough about varying models of the different brands, and their prices. The fast talker seemed to know her own mind and to have some insight into the minds of manufacturers. She was hired, and has been relied on ever since.

The Market Intelligence Unit's first job is to give the Research Department as complete a picture as possible of the choice which might face the shopper who is thinking of buying, say, a washing machine. Since there are usually far more brands than any *Which?* report could deal with, Rebecca's Unit had to find out which were the most commonly found in the shops. And to this had to be added details about where the more obscure models could be bought, which models might be going out of production; price; and how the models varied.

All this demands great accuracy, persistence and tact – *Which?* was not most manufacturers' favourite organisation. And it also demanded generosity of mind on the part of the manufacturers who filled in the enormous questionnaires.

Once the project officers had chosen the brands they were going to test, the sewing machines or the dog food, or whatever it was, had to be bought in such a way that neither manufacturer nor shopkeeper knew that it was going to be tested by *Which?* Even if they had known, it is difficult to see what they could have

Rebecca Wolf, head of the Market Intelligence Unit since 1963

David Watts, now editor of *Which?* as well as *Money Which?*

Edith Rudinger, now editor Consumer Publications and of this book

David Holloway, editor *Handyman Which?* since 1972

done about it, but *Which?* was taking no chances, and the test samples were bought as though by ordinary shoppers. For this, Rebecca organised a Shopping Unit, under a succession of young women called Jenny – Jenny Anderson, then Jenny Prior, now Jenny Huckle – consisting at first of energetic freelances, often resting actors or actresses. Their profession sometimes came in useful, as when one, with a figure like a wand, had to ask for twelve different brands of slimming foods from incredulous shopkeepers. Or when another, large and matronly, had to give the full engineering specifications of six brands of lawn-mower, and insist on all of them.

With something like £150,000 a year being spent on buying the goods for testing, there are now 'professional shoppers' on the staff. They work from home, and include former staff members with babies, and some retired men who are genuine d-i-y specialists. There are also over 100 local shoppers thoughout England, Scotland and Wales who get estimates for work or services in their area and check what is available locally ('my husband is thinking of buying a sun-roof, could you tell me which brands you have and what they cost, please?').

The MIU is a trouble-shooting part of CA in the early stages of any project and is the link between the research department staff and manufacturers or retailers. Part of the Unit's work, now, is to keep continuously under review nearly 30 groups of products such as small and large consumer durables – kettles and irons, washing machines, freezers, cookers, electic drills, lawn mowers, loudspeakers and other hi-fi equipment and so on.

This updating system is now part of CA's continuous batch testing, but was started in order to feed the local consumer advice centres with the up-to-date product information they need. The information stored away in the Market Intelligence Unit's files, shortly to be computerised, can give details of what consumer durables have been on the market, model for model, price for price, over the last 8 years.

The Market Intelligence Unit, which has no parallel in any other consumer organisation, is one of the foundations on which *Which?* rests. Like other foundations, it's largely out of sight, but one would soon notice if it developed a crack. In 20 years, it has not.

The Survey Unit

CA set up the Survey Unit, inside its Research Department, in 1970, and extracted Caroline Collis from her job in an advertising agency to head it. She became one of CA's special people, and still is, in their memory. She died in 1975, aged 44.

Which? tested products under test conditions, usually in a laboratory, to find out as much as possible about their quality and performance. This was most of what people wanted. But it was not enough for finding out how convenient they were to use in a house or kitchen, nor how well people liked them, nor the odd difficulties that some people might find. And it would not show how well a car or a washing machine would stand up to years of use. So the Survey Unit was set up, to do both jobs, collecting the experience, mainly of members, with their vacuum cleaners, electric drills, sewing machines, shampoos, gas cookers. It helped to meet Jennifer Jenkins' constant criticism, when she was Chairman, that our tests were all carried out, under ideal conditions, by men, while the things were used by women, with six jobs to do at once, and children round their feet.

The Survey Unit also met, to a large extent, the criticism that *Which?* could not tell you how long a product would last. From laboratory tests you cannot. But from experience in use, you can, and *Which?*'s annual Car Buying Guide, for example, based on the experience of about 22,000 car-owning members, is an accurate index to the reliability of different brands and models of car.

For investigating services, the Survey Unit was – and remains

– essential. You cannot put solicitors, or a taxi-service, in a laboratory. To find how well a service works, you have to ask the people who use it. So, for example, to discover whether gas servicing is as awful as people say, the Survey Unit asked 900 members for their experience of conversion to natural gas, while it was taking place. (It turned out not to be awful: on the contrary.) To discover whether the servicing of electrical goods was, in general, satisfactory and which firms were best, and worst, the Survey Unit questioned members as a matter of routine.

But the Survey Unit has a use beyond the rounding out of product testing and the investigation of services, most of which need only the experience of members. Its techniques can be used to discover the experience, the opinions and the needs of people in general – far beyond the *Which?* membership. So, for instance, when *Which?* was investigating NHS Maternity Services, the Survey Unit investigated a sample of the whole population, knowing that the experiences of *Which?* members would not necessarily be typical. And when *Which?* was finding out about attitudes to the Common Market, the Survey Unit used two separate samples, suspecting that people in general might feel differently from *Which?* members – as indeed they did.

This aspect of the Survey Unit's work can't be emphasised too strongly. CA cannot claim that its members are typical of the public in general, nor that what they think represents public opinion. But, through the Survey Unit, they can find out, on specific subjects, what most people have experienced, and think and feel, and can use the information when they want to conduct a campaign or press for a reform.

I think people now know the general lines of a Survey Unit's technique. You take a sample of a population, make sure that it is properly representative of that population either by being properly stratified according to age, sex, income, occupation, geographical region, or by being truly random. If properly constituted, even a small-seeming sample (say, 2,000) can represent the experience, opinion or feeling of several millions, with reasonable accuracy. But the questions asked (in interviews or by questionnaire) have to be skilfully designed and carefully analysed. Caroline, leaving an astonished advertising agency behind her, set highly professional standards for the Survey Unit, and enlisted an Advisory Panel, which still keeps an eye on its techniques and performance. Members fill in very long questionnaires (for which they get somewhat inadequate thanks in *Which?*) and the response rate, in general, is more than respectably high – almost always over 60 per cent and often 80–90 per cent. You might say that Caroline built in this window on the world for *Which?*. The present staff keep the panes well polished.

As products become better, their reliability becomes more important. The washing machine or the car, or the tumble drier will do the job, but for how long? And what servicing and repair will be required? The Survey Unit's work in these areas, constantly monitoring members' experiences with the more common consumer durables, is becoming increasingly important to CA. And at the same time, the Survey Unit's role as an independent survey research institute is growing. The Unit offers advice consultancy and survey research to local and central governments, charities, educational and independent research institutes and similar bodies. In some circumstances, work is undertaken under the auspices of CA's associated charitable institution, the Research Institute for Consumer Affairs.

From the The Survey Unit's brochure: *The following projects, recently carried out by the survey unit, give an indication of the range of our work:*

Children in Hospital

Published in 1980 as CA's contribution to the International Year of the Child, this study investigated the facilities for, and attitudes to, children in hospital. Interviews were conducted with parents of recently-hospitalised children, with hospital staff at all levels and, of course, with children. The study was the subject of a paper presented by The Survey Unit at the 1981 Conference of the Association for the Care of Children in Hospital, in Toronto.

Consumer Monitor

A methodological study to examine ways in which the needs of consumers, throughout the EEC, might be assessed. The study was the subject of a paper presented by The Survey Unit at the 1982 Congress of the European Society for Opinion and Marketing Research, held in Vienna.

Towards democracy

From *Financial Times*, 21 March 1959: *The government has decided that the whole problem of consumer protection should be investigated by a special committee. Its terms of reference and composition will be announced as soon as possible, Mr. John Rodgers, Parliamentary Secretary, Board of Trade, told the Commons yesterday.*

From *Hansard* (House of Commons), 27 July 1959: Mr. Rodgers: *I think that we must first try to understand the task that confronts the Committee. It is not the kind of Committee whose main function is merely to elicit facts and views. There are committees which are set up whose job it is to collect all available evidence on a particular subject, to tabulate it and to clearly state what are the facts of the problem. On such committees experts on the subject are appointed and that is the quickest way of getting the job concluded.*

The facts and views which have been expressed so freely in recent years on this subject could reasonably enough be put together without going to the trouble of setting up a committee. The problem is rather this: that the same set of facts in this field produce widely differing views about the appropriate solution – views which I think we must all recognize are for the most part honestly and passionately held by those who propound them.

From *Manchester Guardian*, 1 August 1959: *Lines of inquiry to be followed by the Committee on Consumer Protection were given by the chairman, Mr. J. P. Molony, QC, after its first meeting yesterday. He indicated that the Committee was ready to receive representations.*

From *News Chronicle*, 28 November 1959: *The Government-sponsored committee on consumer protection wants more evidence from the housewife about shoddy goods. It wants to know about shirts that shrink, children's sandals that come unstitched in a day or two, furniture that is warped.*

Yesterday a spokesman for the committee, set out by the Government under J. P. Molony, QC, said: "We would welcome more evidence from housewives."

From *Consumer Information and Protection*, evidence submitted to the Departmental Committee on Consumer Protection by Consumers' Association, March 1960: *In submitting this evidence to the Committee on Consumer Protection, we would like to make it clear that we have for the most part confined ourselves to the seventh in the Committee's own list of subjects to be considered, namely the future of consumer advice and representation, since the experience of the Consumers' Asociation is here particularly relevant. . . . If there is a point we would stress, it is how very greatly we value our independence, which we consider to be the main reason for such success as we have enjoyed.*

From *New Statesman*, 14 May 1960: *The evidence submitted to the Molony Committee on consumer protection mounts steadily, some of it inevitably repetitive. By the time the committee finally reports in 1962, the government will have little excuse for inaction in meeting a general demand for a consumer's organisation sponsored by public funds. From the detailed evidence submitted by, among others, the invaluable Retail-Trading Standards Association and the Consumers' Association, it emerges that much can be done within existing legislation to detect and prosecute sharp practice by manufacturers.*

From the final report of the Committee on Consumer Protection, July 1962 (*the Molony Report*), paragraph 388: *It must also be said that we view with a certain amount of misgiving the (Consumers') Association's oligarchic and self-perpetuating form of government. We fully recognise that its day-to-day management must not be subject to pettifogging supervision if the quality and progress of its operation are to be maintained. We are satisfied that those who control the Association are honest people; that the Association is efficiently run and provides no greater rewards for its employees than their efforts deserve; and that control will not knowingly be handed on to others who are not of like kind. But there can be no guarantee that this body with powerful and ever-growing influence will not one day pass under the direction of persons who might lack the sound judgement of the present hierarchy. Should this occur, we doubt if the danger signal will at once shine clearly.*

We cannot confidently share the belief of the present management that subscribers – who have come to regard Consumers' Association as something of a national institution – would automatically apply the necessary discipline by withdrawing their custom. The concentration of so much power in so few hands must inevitably give rise to concern, and we urge the Association to find the means to introduce a more democratic element into its method of self-government.

From CA's annual report for the year ended 31 March 1962: *We accept the committee's comments that the constitution of CA is by no means ideal. The fact remains that we have not yet been able to find a satisfactory alternative, although both the Council and the Annual General Meetings have repeatedly addressed themselves to the problem. We do not believe that a more democratic constitution for an organisation like ours would necessarily offer effective protection against misuse of the power which comparative testing can give to the Council and to senior members of the staff. There are many examples of institutions with democratic constitutions where power was abused.*

Nevertheless, we shall continue to seek ways in which our constitution can be improved.

Originally we framed our constitution in its present form because we wished to guard against the danger that CA might be captured by groups not sympathetic to its basic aims. Although this danger is probably more remote, we do believe that it has not altogether disappeared. . . .

The expected establishment of a Consumer Council by the Government makes the need for a powerful independent and democratically controlled ginger group greater than ever. The opinions expressed by a more democratically elected CA Council would carry more weight.

From CA's Annual Report for the year ended 31 Marsh 1964: *In June 1963, the Council decided that efforts should be made to increase the number of Ordinary Members. Invitations were therefore sent to 56 individuals who had shown a constructive interest in consumer affairs, and 43 acceptances were received. At the moment there are 143 Ordinary Members. The number will be increased again during the present year.*

From CA's 1965 handbook: *The Council is elected by CA's Ordinary Members who can vote at the Annual General Meeting. There are 154 Ordinary Members at present. Ordinary Membership is at the invitation of the Council. The members of the Council retire by rotation, but may be re-elected.*

From *The Observer*, 12 June 1966: *The Consumers' Association is going democratic – four years after being criticised by the Molony Committee on consumer protection for its method of self-government.*

From *The Guardian*, 28 June 1966: *The Consumers' Association is to increase the number of its voting members from the present maximum of 200 to around 20,000, its chairman, Mrs. Roy Jenkins, announced at the annual general meeting last night. She said voting rights would be offered to long-term supporters of* Which? *– those who have subscribed for at least three years.*

From CA's 1967 handbook, quoting Michael Young: *In 1967 they introduced into their method of election a more democratic element, by inviting any subscriber of three or more years consecutive standing to apply for the vote – in technical terms, to be an Ordinary Member. The purpose of this reform, in the words of CA's Chairman, was to 'strengthen CA's voice as an independent champion of the consumer'.*

From *Which?*, 8 June 1967, page 163: *CA's Council have decided that a greater measure of democratic control should now be introduced. They therefore invite Associate Members, who would like to become voting members and have subscribed for the past three or more years, to apply for Ordinary Membership. Applications will be considered by the Council, and formal invitations will be sent out later. . . .*

Here are a few important points to note:

Ordinary Membership is personal and non-transferable. In the case of families, applications may be signed by either husband or wife, in whose name the voting membership will stand. Companies, public bodies and bulk subscribers may not become voting members. Ordinary Members with managerial responsibilities in manufacture, trade or advertising have never been, and will still not be, eligible to become Council members.

From *Which?*, September 1981, page 539: *Ordinary members are entitled to take part in the Association's affairs at General Meetings, they nominate and elect members of the Council who decide CA's policy, and all Council members are drawn exclusively from their ranks.*

At CA's last Annual General Meeting, Ordinary Members supported the Council's proposals for an increase in their number. There are now about 2,800 Ordinary Members, and we should like to have still more by our next AGM at the end of October.

All paid-up subscribers may now apply. The Council have also waived, as an experiment, payment of the additional Ordinary Membership fee – though, of course, Ordinary Members will continue to be charged the full subscription price for their magazine. It is hoped that these changes will encourage many more of you to participate in CA's affairs.

Consumers' Association

14 Buckingham Street
London WC2N 6DS
01-839 1222

A non-profit company limited by guarantee registered in England. Registered number 580 28
Registered office 14 Buckingham Street London WC2N 6DS

Dear Member

Which? wouldn't be anything like as useful as it is without the help we get from members such as you. Tens of thousands every year tell us what they want in the magazine: say how interested they are in each item in each issue: answer questions ranging from the reliability of their cars to their daily consumption of cornflakes: and liberally respond to our almost monthly cry 'Help wanted'.

The same is true of CA's campaigns. We find out from surveys which consumer issues concern our members most. Our research into monopoly services and public policies draws heavily on their experience. And many of them join in the fight to get deficiencies remedied or laws changed by using CA Action Kits - on e.g. children in hospital, the cost of clothing, food prices, shop hours and (most recently and dramatically) car imports.

This active involvement of our members is a powerful and unique resource for the consumer movement. Now there is one further respect in which we invite it - and that is in helping to elect the governing Council of CA.

When I first joined the Council, back in 1966, the total electorate was under 200. But the following year we became more democratic, and the number of our voting members has gradually climbed to over 2,500. In this Silver Jubilee year we are looking for a fresh advance. At a time when our growing activities as an independent champion of the consumer are more than ever necessary, an expanded electorate could help to give CA a stronger mandate and greater clout.

Would you like to help us in this way?

All you need do is drop a brief note to me personally at the above address, to arrive as soon as possible but not later than 23 August. Quote your membership number or enclose a recent wrapper from your copy of Which?, and clearly mark the envelope AVM in the top left-hand corner. Then, provided you are a fully paid-up individual subscriber to Which? - and not someone in receipt of a company, corporate, bulk or gift subscription - you will be registered as an Associate Voting Member. As long as you stay on the register, you'll be entitled to vote in Council elections.

Each year some of CA's Council either retire or come up for re-election. Candidates may be nominated by Ordinary Members and must themselves be Ordinary Members of CA. (For how an Associate Member can become an Ordinary Member, see Which? September 1981, page 539.) If there are more candidates nominated for the Council than there are vacancies, we hold a postal ballot, and the voters make their choice under the single transferable vote system of proportional representation. From this year, for the first time, every individual member in good standing and duly registered will be able to participate.

I very much hope that you will respond to this invitation.

Yours sincerely,

Rachel Waterhouse

Rachel Waterhouse
Chairman

back page of *Which?* June 1982.

Michael Young

The five chairmen

Michael Young was CA's first chairman, he took over the idea of *Which?* from Dorothy Goodman and I hope I have said enough about him to make it clear that CA could not have survived without him any more than a baby can without a mother or a nurse. I doubt whether Michael was ever very much interested in washing machines or paint strippers or insurance policies. What he cared about most – his mother once told me – was that people should not be poor. He certainly cared that they should not be unhappy. The only time I ever passed the station I should have got out at was reading his *Family and Kinship in East London* and coming to the bit where a young wife sat on the stairs in her new house in a new town and cried her heart out because she wasn't back home in the East End, so the train went on and I with it. Perhaps it was the intellectual toughness required that appealed to him, combined with the feeling that CA's aim was to give ordinary people more confidence and economic power, more equality. I don't know.

From a press release issued by Consumers Association 7 August 1958: *Dr. Michael Young, founder-chairman of the Association, is leaving for America in September. He has accepted an invitation to spend up to a year at the Centre for Advanced Study at Stanford, California.*

The Chairman-elect of the Association is Mrs. Mary Adams OBE, for many years a leading member of the staff of the BBC where she was in charge of TV Talks.

Mary Adams, ex-BBC, took over briefly from Michael Young early on and resigned (but not from the Council) when he came back. Her great contributions were to induce a reluctant BBC to produce the first consumer programme that gave brand names and ratings, and a nervous *Which?* to produce the first comparative test on contraceptives.

Jennifer Jenkins succeeded Michael Young and was chairman for over ten years, resigning about a year before her husband, Roy Jenkins, became president of the EEC Commission.

Jennifer was a notably efficient chairman. Council meetings during her reign ended promptly instead of going on late into the night as with Michael. I think that the director, Peter Goldman, must most of all be grateful for the support he always got through every crisis. The editor at times had mixed feelings. When the chairman bought a *Which?* 'Best Buy' tumbler drier, or night storage heater, or cheap radio for the children, and something went wrong with it, we would hear about it, at length. But I would say now that *Which?* was lucky to have her as chairman for so long. She was married with three children, ran a house with practically no help as far as we could see, had an acute, critical mind, and kept us constantly aware of what people actually needed, practically, from the domestic equipment which we submitted to our laborious tests. We were also very fond of Jennifer.

Christopher Zealley, a trustee of the Dartington Hall Trust has been associated with Michael Young for years. He told me that what most struck new Council members when they joined was the large number of staff, and the high level of their expertise, their professionalism. The staff would be surprised at the council members' surprise; they know that *Which?* needs professionalism to survive.

Christopher Zealley would consider that his main contribution to CA was his interest in the business and administration side and at the same time (which seems contradictory) his encouragement of what he calls the fringe of the consumer movement,

Mary Adams with Peter Goldman

Jennifer Jenkins

Christopher Zealley

Rachel Waterhouse

meaning the campaigns, and CA's support of organisations such as Charles Medawar's Social Audit.

Christopher Zealley encouraged CA in its follow-up to reports. Too often (in his view) *Which?* uncovered a scandal and then lost interest, going on to next month's issue and forgetting the present. For him Action Kits – notably the one on cars – were just right: the practical follow-up to an exposé, a counter-challenge to a powerful lobby. and financial benefit to British motorists.

Rachel Waterhouse lives in, and writes books about, Birmingham, has four children, a husband who researches in cancer statistics, and is CA's present chairman. Concerned to represent real basic consumer interests, she has established herself as a very intelligent and perceptive Council member who did not speak all that often but was listened to respectfully when she did. She is generous, good-humoured and quick to relate the consumer interest to national issues and has been a natural choice for an independent voice on the Price Commission, the National Economic Development Council, the Consumer Consultative Committee to the Commission of the EEC, where she is listened to with the same respect as she gets from the CA Council.

left: Caroline Collis (with her daughter), who set up the Survey Unit. She died in 1975.

below left: Anthony Dumont, who died in 1975, at the age of 58. His signature is among the founder members on CA's Memorandum and Articles of Association, which he had drafted. He served on CA's Council for 22 years.

below right: Paul Fletcher, who died in 1980, after 23 years on CA's Council. He was one of the founder-members and it was he who thought of the title *Which?* for the magazine.

Campaigning, and the law

"This contract is so one-sided" said the learned judge of an agreement produced in court, "that I am surprised to see it written on two sides of the paper".

CA's job through *Which?* is to give people information, for which they have asked, and for which they are willing to pay. It is not to look after them, do good to or protect them. But, inevitably, as time went on, the idea penetrated that there were some short-cuts to getting better value from traders who sold goods and services, and that the short-cuts would provide better value for everyone, not merely CA members.

The idea came naturally from the testing. Very early on, CA investigated the services of dyers and cleaners and found that most customers got on the back of their ticket an agreement in small print when they took anything to be cleaned. The agreement freed the cleaner of all responsibility for the garment's being lost or damaged or for any delay in its return. All the risk was the customer's, none the cleaner's. CA then published the names of cleaners who imposed no conditions (the fairest arrangement for the customer) and others whose conditions were reasonably fair, recommending members to go to no others.

Soon afterwards, the members of the National Federation of Dyers and Cleaners modified their standard agreements and eventually abandoned the small-print conditions and thus accepted responsibility for any loss, damage or delay when they accepted garments for cleaning. CA members benefited, but so did everyone else. In this at least CA was spreading its usefulness beyond its members.

A Consumer Council, at last

At about this time, the Molony Committee on Consumer Protection suggested that CA should be left alone to get on with its job of comparative testing for its members, but that a Consumer Council should be set up to look after the interests of consumers in general, particularly as far as their legal rights were concerned. CA welcomed the Molony report, and the Consumer Council later set up by the Conservative government, with relief and pleasure. CA wanted nothing better than to be left alone by any government; and a government body would be more competent to see that consumers' existing rights were preserved (there were not all that many) and that necessary new legislation was brought in. The Consumer Council appointed as its director Elizabeth Ackroyd, who had been director of the Steel and Power division of the Economic Commission for Europe and a member of the U.K. delegation to the European Coal and Steel Commission and was known as the Iron Lady before Mrs. Thatcher was heard of.

CA and the Consumer Council got on amiably, doing their separate jobs, for eight years, until 1971 when, to general dismay, another Conservative government abolished it. CA was particularly dismayed. They were in a position to know how important the Consumer Council's work had been. Someone had to carry on with the job of seeing that consumers in general were given all the help which the law can give them to take the bitter

---

From CA's evidence to the Departmental Committee on Consumer Protection (Molony Committee), paragraph 54 of evidence: *We recommend that a National Consumers' Council should be set up. Such a Council should not include people who are in any way connected with industry, commerce, advertising or market research. We should be glad to be represented on a Council so constituted.*

---

taste out of the phrase *caveat emptor*. For the time being 'someone' had to be CA.

The consumer and the law

At this point, we have to go back a little and bring in David Tench.

In 1962 (as I have mentioned) CA had decided to publish a simple book explaining consumer law and had given the job of editing it to Edith Rudinger. She looked around for a lawyer who was willing to write it and had some free evenings and weekends, and finally found David Tench in Inland Revenue. She required 30,000 words, in six weeks, and since he had never written a word before, except to defaulting taxpayers, he did not know that the request was an outrageous one. In fact, he never discovered it. *The law for consumers* was successful immediately. It was followed by *Law for motorists* and *Wills and Probate* and *The legal side of buying a house*.

They were successful because they were absolutely simple, usable guides, without hedging or qualification, which anyone could follow, and which showed the way out of everyday legal difficulties. *The legal side of buying a house* was also a simple guide, showing that you can do your own conveyancing, and how to do it, so saving sizeable lawyers' fees. But it was also the first assault on the lawyers' monopoly of conveyancing. It was seen as a blow for consumers, against a professional monopoly – part of a fight.

By 1969 David Tench was embedded in CA and Peter Goldman

From *Which?* January 1964 page 3: *As you see, we have given one page in* Which? *to the* National Consumer Council *to say in it exactly what they choose. The Consumer Council pay our printer for the typesetting of the page, but they do not pay us. They will have this page each month for six months – to see how the arrangement works – and they will have full editorial control over it, not even telling us beforehand what they are going to say.*

This is a most unusual thing for us to do, obviously. We have done it because we believe in the Consumner Council and hope, for all our sakes, that it will succeed.

---

invited him to regularise the position by joining the staff, which would at least give him his weekends and evenings to himself. His job thereafter was to see that the law was changed, in the consumer's favour, wherever it was necessary and possible, and to use *Which?*'s research, where appropriate, to do this.

Tench, like those officers whom generals prefer, is lucky, and on the day he started his new job, found that *Which?* had published a report on Unsolicited Goods. The problem was that people often got through the post goods (such as books or records) which they had not ordered and did not want. Legally, they could not be obliged to pay for them but were not allowed to damage or get rid of them. Most people did not know this and many (particularly the poor and old) paid, through fear. Even those who did not pay were nervous at having the things around. The report included a CA member's suggestion that CA should sponsor a Private Member's Bill allowing anyone who received such goods to get rid of them if the sender did not collect them within a reasonable time. "Ha," said David Tench, and drafted the bill.

This was the first bill that David Tench had ever drafted. He knew enough, since there was a Labour government at the time, to enlist the support of Arthur Davidson, a Labour MP high on the ballot list for private members' Bills. The draft *Inertia Selling Bill* sailed merrily along, a small, simple reform opposed by no one who mattered, and by May 1970 seemed certain to become law, when the Labour government fell and the Conservatives came in. Lucky Tench found that Philip Goodhart, the Conservative MP on CA's council, was second in the ballot for private members' Bills and persuaded him to take it on. This is how David Tench describes it:

Unsolicited Goods and Services Act 1971

This Act gives a consumer who has been sent an article which he does not want and has not asked for the right to dispose of it without legal problems. Before then, although he was not legally bound to pay for it, he could not readily rid himself of some legal responsibility for it. He had no right to throw it away, for example. This Act gave him the right to throw it away, or use it as his own, after 6 months in any event, or after 30 days, on giving notice to the sender that they were unsolicited goods. It also made it an offence knowingly to demand payment for what were known to be unsolicited goods.

Based on CA research published in *Which?* for June 1969, it was CA's first legislative achievement.

A Minister for Consumer Affairs

At this stage, the government abolished the Consumer Council. A year later, as though realising that this had been a bad mistake and an unpopular one, it appointed Sir Geoffrey Howe as Minister for Consumer Affairs within the Department of Trade and Industry.

Peter Goldman, CA's director, had in 1970 publicly advocated a minister of consumer affairs. The idea originated with the creation of a Department of Consumer and Corporate Affairs in Canada. Peter Goldman visited Ottowa for talks with the Minister and his officials in January 1970, and was won over. In May 1970, winding up CA's special seminar for Ordinary Members, Peter Goldman outlined what was lacking here institutionally, and what was wanted. Jennifer Jenkins, CA's chairman, spelt out at the 1971 Annual General Meeting that it was CA's policy to press for a Minister for Consumer Affairs. Sir Geoffrey Howe was appointed in 1972. (And Michael Young told the 1974 Annual General Meeting that he had been sceptical of the original proposal but totally converted by its practical results.)

From CA's Annual Report for the year ended March 1976: *Since 1973 we have experimented with a subscription-based Personal Service. Having won its laurels, it will now be promoted to members, though initially on a modest scale.*

There are now over 6000 members subscribing to *Which? Personal Service*. The staff includes three solicitors and two barristers, under Beryl Johnson who is now the Head of Advisory Services. She started working at CA in 1962.

Sir Geoffrey was energetic and appeared to believe in what he was doing. He got through the Supply of Goods (Implied Terms) Act, 1973, which put an end to the scandal of the small print which attempts to take way the customer's right of redress when goods are faulty. He got throught the important Fair Trading Act (which outlaws many doubtful business practices) and set up the Office of Fair Trading (which sees that the Act is obeyed). He was the moving spirit behind the setting up of the Small Claims procedures in county courts in 1973 (which made it easier for consumers with complaints to get the redress to which they were entitled). CA had campaigned for effective consumer redress by legal means for many years and was involved in the negotiation which led to the change in the county court rules (no Act of Parliament was needed) that led to the present system. At first only cases involving up to £75 were covered. Later this sum was raised to £100, then to £200 and finally to the present level of £500. The scheme has been a considerable success.

In 1974 the Heath goverment fell. Shirley Williams became Minister for Consumer Affairs, with her own independent department and a seat in the Cabinet, and in 1975 set up the National Consumer Council, with a small budget, Michael Young as Chairman and John Hosker, ex-Head of Information of CA, as director. CA went round Brussels boasting that that UK had the only consumer Cabinet Minister in the Common Market, and the government passed the Consumer Credit Act.

Briefly, the Act required that hire purchase traders must be licensed and that customers must be told the real amount of the interest that they would be paying. The second point was dear to CA's heart. Years before, in its third issue, *Which?* had discovered to its horror that, while the presumably well-off customers of some of the classier stores paid no interest when they bought something on hire purchase, a man who had bought a bicycle in a suburban shop had paid 69 per cent. Normally, the customers had no idea of what interest they were paying. He or she would see the cash price, the deposit and the amount and number of weekly or monthly instalments. If they remembered to deduct the deposit and could do the arithmetic to find the total amount they would pay, they could work out the percentage rate of interest on what they were borrowing. But in fact fewer than half the population can work out a percentage. And even then the real rate of interest would be roughly double, because the sum of money they owe is diminishing all the time. Very few customers indeed would realise this. Hence CA's continuing enthusiasm for legislation which required that the arithmetic must be done by the trader.

Consumer Credit Act 1974

This Act brought into law the main recommendations of the Crowther Committee on consumer credit. This committee had been set up in 1969, and CA had submitted a powerful case to it for a comprehensive measure to regulate consumer credit by law. In particular, CA had been in the forefront of a campaign to require those who lend money and provide credit to state the true rate of interest.

The Consumer Credit Act 1974 is the longest and most comprehensive of the pieces of consumer legislation passed in the 1970s. The sweeping reforms it has introduced have proved formidable to implement. But two most important principles which CA called for are now in force: the licensing of all businesses in any way involved in the providing of credit, and the truth in lending provision.

In the meantime, on an entirely different scale, David Tench fathered an Act that arose naturally out of the work he had done in connection with the Consumer Publication *How to sue in the county court.*

Litigants in Person (Costs and Expenses) Act 1975

This Act was promoted by CA, taken up by the Rt Hon. Arthur Bottomley MP (Labour, Middlesborough). It gives a person who sues successfuly as a litigant in person in the civil courts the right to recover legal costs against his opponent, to compensate for some of the time and effort he puts into bringing and winning the case.

The third from the left is David Tench, in 1973, when *How to sue in the county court* was published.

If the winner in a court case involving more than £500 was represented by a solicitor, then the solicitor's costs of preparing the case (poring over documents, copying, and so on) are part of the costs payable by the loser. If the winner does this himself – that is, as a litigant in person – he could not recover these costs from the other side. This discrimination against lay litigants in person was the main reason for CA (in the form of David Tench) being spurred into action. It was at a time when consumer legislation was, by and large, coming from government sources and was a bit off-beat, so far as main consumer issues were concerned. The rest of the CA staff took a lot of persuading on that one; but supported Tench's work on what became the important Unfair Contract Terms Act.

Unfair Contract Terms Act 1977

This was CA's most significant legislative achievement. It finally knocked on the head the evils of small print in exclusion clauses in contracts and notices. It was based on Law Commission work, and completed the work begun by Supply of Goods (Implied Terms) Act 1973. The 1977 Act introduced controls in relation to the law of negligence and in relation to services. It says that where personal injury or death may be involved, a purported exclusion or restriction on liability is completely invalid. In other cases (in contracts involving services, or where questions of negligence affecting property rather than life and limb are concerned, the small print is only legally effective if the trader can prove that it is fair and reasonable.

This Bill was promoted by CA, taken up by Mr Michael Ward MP (Labour, Peterborough) who came 13th in the ballot in November 1976. It ought to have been a government Bill, as it was

From Hansard (House of Lords), 23 May 1977, 4.58 pm: Lord Denning: *My Lords, I am sorry that I was not in my place when the noble Lord, Lord Jacques, moved the Second Reading (of the Unfair Contracts Terms Act). It seems to me to introduce one of the most important reforms in our time in our civil law, both of contract and of tort. . . .*

a long and complicated issue. It was squeezed out of the government programme by Scottish devolution. So, CA inspired a private member's Bill. To our surprise and delight, it succeeded, having been blessed at a fairly early stage with government support from the then Minister of State for Consumer Affairs, John Fraser MP.

Consumer Safety Act 1978

By 1977 it had become apparent that the Consumer Protection Act 1971 was a very inadequate legal basis for providing compulsory safety standards for consumers. The Consumer Protection Act 1971 had been rushed through Parliament on an emergency basis, following a number of horror stories about unsafe oil heaters. The Government decided in the mid-1970s that a comprehensive consumer safety measure was required, but no legislative time had been found. In the autumn of 1977, CA made this its main campaigning issue, and Mr Neville Trotter MP (Conservative, Tynemouth) who did well in the ballot, took it up at our invitation. It went through with Government support.

One down, two to go

In 1979 the government changed again.

Which? had found out long before that most people wanted shops to stay open as long as they (the shops) liked. (The Union of Shop, Distributive and Allied Workers did not.) In 1980, CA's attempt to get a Shops Hours Bill through was talked out.

At this stage, the detached friendliness existing between CA and the National Consumer Council grew into something closer. There was no reason for rivalry between them since CA's

---

From CA's Annual Report for the year ended March 1981: *And in the county court at Exeter, David Tench representing a subscriber to* Which? Personal Service *is to succeed in challenging unfair 'small print' in a service contract.*

---

main job was comparative testing and the National Consumer Council's was to do everything they could for the consumer *except* comparative testing. (And many of the Council's senior staff including its present director, Jeremy Mitchell, had begun their consumer career with CA.) In an official climate which was, to say the least, cool about consumer interests, they huddled together for warmth and decided to collaborate in an attempt to get more safeguards for consumers.

Supply of Goods and Services Act 1982

This Act extends the kind of protection provided for consumers by the Sale of Goods Act to cases where consumers acquire goods not by cash purchase – for example, in the course of a repair, by a hiring agreement, on an exchange of goods. It also codifies basic legal rights in relation to contracts for services, making it clear that the consumer has the right to have services carried out with reasonable care and skill, within a reasonable time and (unless a price is agreed) at a reasonable price.

All these rights already existed under the common law, so that the act codifies what was already the law. Thus, although there was no actual change in consumers' legal rights, it is a very useful clarification of existing rights.

The Act follows a Law Commission report (on goods) and the National Consumer Council's report (on services) published in October 1981, entitled *Service Please*. CA had put forward the Law Commission's proposal in November 1980 as one of several possible private member's Bills, but there were no takers then. In November 1981, CA and the NCC put forward this reform as a joint proposal. Then no less than three MPs in the top twenty in the ballot expressed interest in this proposal, two of them responding to CA, one to the NCC. In the event, the NCC took responsibility for the Supply of Goods and Services Bill while CA took primary responsibility for seeing another Bill, the Food and Drugs (Amendment) Bill, through Parliament.

Rosemary McRobert, with Robin Young of *The Times*, July 1982, when the Food and Drugs Amendment Bill received the Royal Assent.

David Tench with Lord Darling of Hillsborough who had the care of the Food and Drugs Amendment Bill in the House of Lords.

Food and Drugs (Amendment) Act 1982

This Act significantly increases the penalties for breaches of food law, increasing the fines from a maximum of £100 to £1000 for convictions in the magistrates courts, and making it possible for serious cases to go to the Crown Court. Time limits for bringing prosecutions are also increased. The Act follows scandals about unfit meat much publicised in 1981 and 1982.

The Act was introduced by Mr Norman Atkinson MP (Labour Tottenham) who came second in the ballot for private members' Bills in November 1981. The Bill received the Royal Assent on 13 July 1982.

It's a long job

I have gone into what may seem long and tedious detail about these Acts of Parliament and private members' Bills because they have become part of CA's work, and because the process of getting them through is indeed long and, in parts, tedious. The law is not an ass, but it often behaves like a mule, and anyone who intends to lead it needs patience, faith and resilience in abundance, and in that order. *Which?* produced its first report on hire purchase charges in the spring of 1958. The Consumer Credit Act came into force sixteen years later. *Which?*'s first report on dyers' and cleaners' agreements was in the summer of 1958. The Supply of Goods (Implied Terms) Act was passed fifteen years later. And so on. David Tench worked patiently on legal documents, thoroughly enjoying himself, while the *Which?* staff, with their monthly deadlines, took little notice of what he was doing, until they woke up to find that another piece of consumer legislation had got on to the statute books and that CA was getting the credit.

Beyond the law: campaigning

CA also has the job of considering consumer interests beyond the scope of immediate Parliamentary Bills. At different times, different things seemed important. There was always so much to do, CA's resources so inadequate to do it all. At times it meant a conscious effort not to be swamped by subjects we find intellectually or technically beguiling.

Some campaigning or representation work is detailed, involving much tenacity over long periods of consultation, sometimes silence and regression, before something – perhaps a change in public opinion or official attitude, or a political change or change in policy – fans the issue into life again. For much of this work, we are the only resource available for the consumer case.

But there are some constants, such as safety, education, consumer representation.

Which?'s first question – about anything electrical, or cars, or whatever was tested, was whether or not it was safe. I think *Which?* could say that it has played a large part with the British Standards Institution in making consumer goods safer than they used to be. In the 1960s we led the field in getting the lead out of children's toys, in the 1980s, we are campaigning to get lead out of petrol. CA acts as a constant scourge and goad on the improvement of standards of safety.

Education was another of CA's campaigning issues. Most consumer organisations worry about consumer education in schools, knowing that if all children were taught how to get value for money, whatever they were buying; how to judge advertisements; how to know their rights; how to apply to their practical life the academic lessons of mathematics and physics and chemistry – if they could do this, then the gap between *Which?* members and the rest of the population might lessen, if not disappear.

From *Which? No. 2*, Winter 1958, page 3: *In the first issue of* Which?, *we published the results of some tests on electric kettles, and made comments on what the tests showed. Among the kettles reviewed was the polished aluminium kettle made by the Co-operative Wholesale Society, which was described as having 'a weakly-constructed handle and a very poor finish to the spout'.*

The Manager of the C.W.S. factory which makes the kettles has now written to tell us that, as a result of the criticism, they are 'substituting a stronger gauge aluminium strip in the handle to strengthen the alleged weakness, and have also taken care to see that the criticism of the spout has been corrected'.

Representation – CA has always believed that the nationalised industries which are, after all, supposed to be run in the public interest, would be more likely to do so in practice, if the public had some effective way of making their voice heard in the way they are run. Britain already has, on paper, a system for achieving this in the consumer councils of the gas, electricity, coal and transport industries and of the post office, airline users and airports. CA has supported the system by nominating consumers to these Councils wherever it can. But the genuine consumer members are heavily outnumbered and technically uninformed. Most of the general public don't even know they exist; the system does not work.

CA knows that the bureaucracy of the nationalised industries, and the way successive governments use them in formulating their policy, is often in conflict with the legitimate expectations of consumers. So the relationship between nationalised industries, government and consumers is an issue that CA hopes to study in a context wider than just the role of the nationalised industries' consumer councils.

From *Handyman Which?* report on chain saws February 1982, page 70: *As part of our test programme, we subjected our saws to a detailed safety check, noting all the safety features present and taking into account the handling of each machine. The results were frightening: we had specific criticisms of nearly every saw. Happily, some of the chain saws we were most critical of have been modified or will be available shortly with modifications.*

From *Which?* June 1982, page 326: *The design of some push chairs leaves much to be desired and you could easily buy an unsafe one. This means that the product safety law is not adequate.*

We welcome the government's review of the Consumer Safety Act and think it should be treated as a matter of urgency. We also think the push chair safety regulations themselves should be brought quickly up to date to cover new push chair designs. We'll keep you informed of any developments in future issues of Which?

Consumer campaigning will go on and on

Representation, information, education and safety – these have been the main headings of CA's campaigning over the years, and there have been successes and failures. On the whole, the story has been one of success, not so much of specific changes in society, as in the slow, but growing, acceptance of these priorities as necessary, and desirable.

What had been lacking, perhaps, was the orderly deployment of part of CA's resources to campaigning purposes, and the persistent following-up of chosen aims. Rosemary McRobert, deputy director of CA, now has charge of this deployment. If anyone can succeed with it, she will. There are research officers specifically assigned to campaigning; a budget; the considerable research resources of CA to draw upon; the links with BEUC, and a programme.

Here are some of the issues it means to tackle, or go on tackling, in the next ten years (quite apart from examining the responsiveness of nationalised industries to consumer needs).

Developments in broadcasting and communication: CA is contributing a consumer view on the way in which the new developments of cable and satellite communications should be managed to give consumers more choice, without throwing away the achievements of public service broadcasting.

Local authorities – are they efficient? Our members are concerned about local authority expenditure, as rate-payers who feel that local authorities may be inefficient and are lacking in accountability; we are undertaking a research project on the way local authorities report their finance and activities.

Information technology and the consumer's right to privacy and protection: the implications of the microchip for the way people lead their lives and have their lives recorded and docketed from cradle to the grave have been part of our consideration for some time. We first took them on board in relation to a report published in *Which?* April 1980 on safeguards for personal information. CA is also involved with the impact on consumers of all aspects of information technology – from the numbering of articles at the point of sale, to the electronic transfer of money.

Consumer advice: a new initiative in reaching a wider public.

Fair trading: the access to legal redress for many consumers is still too difficult and complicated, even when the law provides for their recompense, and the enforcement of existing legislation is patchy. CA is developing ideas on new ways to fill old gaps.

Competition: continuing and extending CA's battle against restrictions in competition, as in the Common Agricultural Policy, monopolies and mergers, air fares. We are often able to spot the signs of anti-competitive practices in our market intelligence for *Which?* reports; singular similarity in prices in shops or advertisements, for example, and we co-operate with the office of Fair Trading by letting them have what evidence we have.

House transfers: CA has nibbled at the subject in the past starting with the breakthrough of *The legal side of buying a house*; now we shall treat it more systematically.

Pressure for legislation on product liability which would mean that anyone injured by a faulty product would be compensated.

Safety; first, last and continuingly. Constant vigilance over safety aspects of our *Which?* tests continue to be an important priority.

This is an ambitious programme, even for ten years, and it may not all be achieved. But it has new things in it. It is orderly. It is not unrealistic.

From the C.E.C.G. pamphlet on *Product Liability the case for Compensation* page 7: *Products rarely cause injury or damage. When they do the victims should be easily and adequately compensated. Damage caused by a defect in a product usually involves a cost which, while often small, must be borne by someone. It is unjust that the particular individual who has had the misfortune to be injured or has otherwise suffered damage because of a defective product should bear the burden alone. A system of strict liability effectively spreads the cost amongst all consumers. There is no evidence that extending strict liability to all goods would increase prices unduly.*

A Planning Committee meeting, in 1982:
left to right: Melvin Coleman (head of finance), Peter Sand (chief scientific officer), Bruce McConnach (head of marketing), Alastair Macgeorge (assistant director), Rosemary McRobert (deputy director), Peter Goldman (the director), Daphne Grose (head of representation), Bill Roberts (assistant director), Sue Read (assistant director), Anthony Land (head of publishing), David Tench (legal officer).

What's to come

CA's income is now around £12 million. Basically, this has been achieved by having certain principles and sticking to them. *Which?* and CA have nothing to sell except information which cannot be obtained elsewhere, which (as far as is humanly possible) can be trusted to be accurate, which is unbiassed, and which is directly and practically useful. Any softening of these principles, and members and income would have vanished.

But principles by themselves are not enough. If an enterprise is to survive a recession and an inflation which have ravaged the businesses of this country, and, what's more, to advance in twenty–five years from a debt of £187 to an annual income of £12 million, the enterprise has to have first class administration and a first class financial policy. CA has, and has had, that.

The most important aim of CA's financial life is to remain solvent. Any surplus must be spent in improving its service to members or forwarding the consumer interest in other ways. If there were no surplus, it would be sad, but not tragic. Only by remaining solvent can CA keep its independence from outside finance and, therefore, from outside interference. It goes without saying that *Which?* takes no advertising and no financial assistance from industry. *Which?* members believe what *Which?* says, largely because they know that CA depends entirely on their subscriptions and is not dependent to any degree on any official or unofficial body, however honourable or benevolent.

Under Peter Goldman's overall direction, CA relies on the financial good sense of the assistant director Alan Hill and on the professionalism and expertise of the head of marketing, Bruce McConnach. The marketing department and the *Which?* editors all agree that the product – *Which?* and its supplements – must be what the members want, not what the editors want to write or the marketing department wants to sell. So *Which?* continually surveys members to find out what products and services they most want tested, which reports they have found useful, which they have not. The result is that over 80 per cent of members renew their subscriptions, which is at once a guarantee that members are getting, on the whole, what they want, and the base on which CA's solid finances rest.

I asked as many people as I could what they wanted for CA in the future, in what direction they would like the organisation to go. Few of them found it easy to answer.

Most were insistent, to begin with, that the research should keep its quality and, if possible, be improved. Even more were concerned that the reports should be in plain English, and that the only direction to move in was to get the English plainer, and the reports more immediately intelligible. After that, the answers were less categorical, and more divergent.

Some were chiefly concerned with CA's financial health. They saw this as coming from a maintained, or improved, service to members combined with active promotion to get as many

---

From the press release launching *Prestel for people*, 18 March 1982: *This is the first time that anyone has got to grips with the problem of bringing information technology to the ordinary man and woman in the street. . . .*

Prestel is the name of British Telecom's viewdata service. It allows information from a computer to be called up over a telephone line and displayed in words, numbers and simple diagrams on a television screen. It can also be used to send messages, order goods and make complaints. Information already available on Prestel includes news, weather, buying advice from Which?, *social security benefits from the DHSS, health advice from the Health Education Council, how to complain from the Office of Fair Trading, and local information from many sources including local councils.*

The project is being managed by CA, publishers of Which? *and providers of the* Telewhich? *service on Prestel.*

---

members, willing to pay an economic price for the service, as possible.

Some, in order to improve this service, look to new ways of getting consumer information to the people who need it – using new information technology.

Some people take for granted that CA will go on looking after its members' interests as well as it can and are more interested in its wider role. They think of it, in one way or another, as caring for the interests of all consumers, not only its members.

Some would like CA to concentrate on the underprivileged. Some would like CA to become much more closely linked with other consumer organisations, in Europe and outside it. Some want CA to concentrate less on consumption, more on conservation.

But the strongest wishes, or at least the most strongly expressed wishes, are for *Which?* to break through the sound barrier – which means that what it has to say should be heard by most people – and, for CA's campaigning to succeed in getting the interests of the consumer to be considered as equal to the interests of industry and of trade unions.

There seems to be enough idealism among the realists of Council and staff, and enough realism among the idealists, to keep each other in perpetual check. This must make life difficult for the chairman and the director, but is healthy for the organisation and its members.

Peter Goldman cutting the *Which?* silver jubilee cake.